Living Service

FT Prentice Hall
FINANCIAL TIMES

In an increasingly competitive world, we believe it's quality of thinking that gives you the edge – an idea that opens new doors, a technique that solves a problem, or an insight that simply make sense of it all. The more you know, the smarter and faster you can go.

That's why we work with the best minds in business and finance to bring cutting-edge thinking and best learning practice to a global market.

Under a range of leading imprints, including *Financial Times Prentice Hall,* we create world-class print publications and electronic products bringing our readers knowledge, skills and understanding, which can be applied whether studying or at work.

To find out more about Pearson Education publications, or tell us about the books you'd like to find, you can visit us at www.pearsoned.co.uk

PEARSON
Education

Living Service

HOW TO DELIVER THE SERVICE OF THE FUTURE TODAY

Marc Silvester and Mohi Ahmed

FT Prentice Hall

FINANCIAL TIMES

An imprint of **Pearson Education**

Harlow, England • London • New York • Boston • San Francisco • Toronto
Sydney • Tokyo • Singapore • Hong Kong • Seoul • Taipei • New Delhi
Cape Town • Madrid • Mexico City • Amsterdam • Munich • Paris • Milan

PEARSON EDUCATION LIMITED

Edinburgh Gate
Harlow CM20 2JE
Tel: +44 (0)1279 623623
Fax: +44 (0)1279 431059
Website: www.pearsoned.co.uk

First published in Great Britain in 2008

ISBN: 978-0-273-71535-1

British Library Cataloguing-in-Publication Data
A catalogue record for this book is available from the British Library

Library of Congress Cataloging-in-Publication Data
Silvester, Marc.
  Living service : how to deliver the service of
the future today / Marc Silvester and Mohi Ahmed.
        p. cm.
  Includes bibliographical references and index.
  ISBN-13: 978-0-273-71535-1 (alk. paper)
                        2. Service industries. I.
Ahmed, Mohi. II. Title.
    HF5415.5.S557 2008
    658. '12--dc22

2008000741

10 9 8 7 6 5 4 3 2 1
10 09 08

Typeset in Plantin 10pt/14pt by 30
Printed and bound in Great Britain by Henry Ling Ltd, Dorchester, Dorset

The publisher's policy is to use paper manufactured from sustainable forests.

Praise for Living Service

"Living Service *will revolutionize service industries in the same way that lean thinking revolutionized manufacturing.*"

Ikujiro Nonaka, author of *The Knowledge-creating Company*, Professor Emeritus of International Business Strategy, ICS-Hitotsubashi University

"*When doing business with Toyota, service providers need to understand our mind, body and soul.* Living Service *shows how this can be done by all service providers in the future.*"

Hiroji Onishi, Managing Officer and CIO, Toyota Motor Corporation

"*To achieve real and sustained continuous improvement in the delivery of IT services you need a different mindset around putting customers first and a different business model that supports that way of thinking.   Fujitsu has both.*"

David Lister, CIO, Reuters

"*In this marvellous book, Marc Silvester and Mohi Ahmed show how and why Fujitsu has long been a leader in creating technology to provide service excellence to its customers. With real examples, such as Toyota and Reuters, the authors show how a dedication to co-creation and living service delivers real and lasting value. Using the metaphor of living service, the authors create a wonderful story of a journey which managers will find uplifting, fascinating, provoking and from which they will learn important business lessons.* Living Service *is a must-read for anyone working in partnerships or interested in co-creation.*"

Professor Lynda Gratton, London Business School

"Innovation in services will be the next wave of innovation. This book provides a very useful perspective on both the art and the science of service innovation."

Professor Henry Chesbrough, author of *Open Innovation*, Executive Director of the Center for Open Innovation, Haas School of Business, University of California, Berkeley.

*"*Living Service *is a revolutionary approach to transforming service industries. Based on insights from both East and West, and the appealing metaphor of the mind, body and soul, it will find applications in many service industries especially in countries such as India as their competitiveness develops."*

Dr. K. Momaya, Chairperson, Strategic Management Group, Department of Management Studies, Indian Institute of Technology (IIT), New Delhi

"A wonderful book showing how the mind, body and soul of all organizations can be brought together in an interconnected whole to help create a sustainable future for us all."

Jin Tatsumura, Director, Gaia Symphony

This book is dedicated to the people who relentlessly pursue living service excellence to build a sustainable future.

Contents

Preface   x

About the authors   xii

Acknowledgements   xiii

Introduction: Inside Living Service   1

Part 1: Mind 心 Kokoro   **29**
1   Developing a Living Service Culture   31
2   Changing the Game   50

Part 2: Body 体 Karada   **63**
3   Engaging with Customers   73
4   Accelerating Customers' Opportunities   85
5   Delivering Great Service   96
6   Co-creating the Future   105

Part 3: Soul 魂 Tamashii   **117**
7   Maximizing Collective Energy   119

Epilogue: Sustaining Service   140

Appendix: Your Living Service Agenda   151

Notes   153

Index   156

Preface

Every book is a journey. This book is about a continuing journey towards living service excellence, a uniquely powerful approach, which allows service providers to transform themselves while sustainably delivering significant benefits to customers and their customers. Throughout this book we aim to articulate the concept of living service, drawing on many stories of service that affect our everyday lives around the world. We also provide pointers showing how other organizations can transform themselves using living service.

The objective of living service is clear: to revolutionize service industries in the same way that 'lean' thinking revolutionized manufacturing. But don't let this bold objective put you off. Like many of the best ideas that have changed the face of business – from total quality management to lean production – living service is based on fundamentally simple – and deliverable – ideas and practices. Living service leverages tacit knowledge embedded in people and is delivered by a combination of art and science that continuously adapts and evolves, both anticipating and responding to customers' needs.

Our experience is that living service offers a powerful competitive edge in services. This approach is already delivering extraordinary benefits to Fujitsu and our customers and their customers. Benefits include 30 per cent faster deployment of services; 30 per cent more reliable services; costs cut by 15 per cent plus; greater consistency, flexibility, scalability, continuous innovation and more business opportunities globally.

In describing the continuing transformation towards living service we use the metaphor of *Mind, Body and Soul*. This metaphor reflects the organic nature of living service, and the powerful combination of theory, practice and inspiration that supports it. To deliver living service, service providers need to understand, honour and respond to the Mind, Body and Soul of their customers throughout the journey.

As we shall see, everyone is in service. All industries have a service component to a greater or lesser extent. Living service draws on knowledge and experience from Japan, Europe, North America and other parts of the world. We believe the living service approach is universal and applicable in any industry sector, discipline and geographic location.

The ideas described in this book are based on our continued collaboration with thousands of people within and outside Fujitsu, and the observation of service transformation across industries over the years. Each chapter of the book is a stepping stone on the way to achieving living service. They offer important pointers for anyone faced with the task of continuously providing great service to their customers. We have tried to draw out the main learning points with agenda items for each chapter.

In the final analysis – indeed, in *any* rational analysis – business is nothing without customers and, in our hypercompetitive times, customers expect great service. We hope that living service will help in your quest to deliver the great service your customers demand and deserve.

Marc Silvester and Mohi Ahmed, London
January 2008

About the Authors

Marc Silvester is Chief Technology Officer of Fujitsu's services organization, based in the UK. Marc leads a global services programme. Previously, he initiated and managed a number of global alliances for Fujitsu and expanded the company's network of global partners. Marc joined Fujitsu in the UK in 1986 as a software engineer and has worked on a wide variety of business transformation projects across the company. He is a graduate of Staffordshire University with an honours degree in pure and applied computer science.

Mohi Ahmed is Director of Strategic Development at Fujitsu's services organization, based in the UK. He joined Fujitsu's corporate HR strategy unit in 2001 having previously worked on the company's executive training programme and for major industrial organizations in Japan, Canada, and the United States. Mohi was named as one of the world's key 'idea practitioners' in Thomas H. Davenport and Laurence Prusak's book *What's the Big Idea?* (Harvard Business School Press, 2003). Mohi has been a visiting scholar at Harvard Business School and ICS-Hitotsubashi University. He has a PhD in communications from Simon Fraser University, Canada.

Acknowledgements

T his book grew out of a journey of discovery – one that has been exciting and sometimes exhausting, but always enlightening and worth the effort. We thought we already knew about service, but we found there is always more to know.

Along the way we have learned from many people inside and outside Fujitsu. To all we are grateful.

First, we would like to thank many people across the Fujitsu Group who inspired us and provided support to this project. They include Naoyuki Akikusa, Ella Bennett, Roger Camrass, David Courtley, Hiromichi Hirata, Kazuo Ishida, Chiaki Ito, Takanori Katayama, Kazuhiko Kato, Tsuneo Kawatsuma, Hiromasa Kimura, Hiroaki Kurokawa, Ron Mitchell, Kazuo Miyata, Yoshi Miyata, Hiroki Nakagiri, Philip Oliver, Kiyoshi Saitou, Yuichi Sakai, Michitaka Sugawara, Kizou Tagomori, Hiroshi Yamamoto, Shingo Yamasaki, Hajime Yoshioka and Toshimasa Wada.

We greatly appreciate the contributions of the champions of change who provided stories to help us explain the living service concept in practice. They include Alison Argyle, Mark Dorgan, Alan Goswell, Rodney Hobbs, Winfried Holz, Toshiyuki Imamura, Keiichi Kato, Glenn Pearce, Jorge Salvador, Steve Saunders, Renate Schwarz, Bill Simpson, Marilyn Slavin, Mark Southcott, Hiroshi Suyama, Ian Terblanche and Steve Walsh.

We received guidance and advice from many others. In particular we thank Ikujiro Nonaka, Professor Emeritus of International Business Strategy at ICS-Hitotsubashi University; Lynda Gratton, Professor of Management Practice at London Business School; and Jin Tatsumura, Director of Gaia Symphony. Their guidance helped us to link theory and practice along with articulating a universal perspective.

We would like to thank our publisher Liz Gooster and the team at Financial Times Prentice Hall who helped us with the manuscript.

Our warmest thanks and appreciation to Stuart Crainer and Des Dearlove of CrainerDearlove for their dedication and support throughout this journey.

We also give our heartfelt thanks to our team: Saeko Awata, Alison Baker, Antony Bellingall, Philippa Bryan, Peter Court, Jat Sahi, Ed Tilsley, Kyoko Yamachika and Shohei Yamada. Supporting us all have been Shukuko, George, Kerry, Jai, Biba and James. Also, we would like to thank the many others who have contributed such valuable insights as we researched, wrote and reviewed the manuscript.

Finally, we would like to thank our families and friends around the world. In particular, Marc would like to thank Lewis, Jack and Juliet. Mohi would like to thank Poplar and Nanako.

Introduction:
Inside Living Service

Do you ever stop to think how much we take for granted in our everyday lives? What were once hailed as technological marvels we now happily accept. What was once an impossible technological dream is now part of the reassuring furniture of day-to-day living. The magical becomes the habitual with daunting ease.

Think about global travel. Thanks to modern aircraft, journeys that once took months or even years now take just a few hours. To an earlier generation, this would have seemed little short of miraculous. Yet we do not even register it as an achievement. When we see an aircraft we do not give it a second thought. We do not worry about what keeps it in the sky or how many people it can carry. But that was not always the case.

Or, think about some of the other conveniences of modern life. Think of modern communications. Using our mobile phones, we expect to be able to contact people anywhere in the world from wherever we happen to be – instantly. When we draw cash from a bank we expect to get it straightaway – in the currency of the country we happen to be in. But that was not always the case either. So why do we take these things for granted?

The reason is bound up with changes in the way these products are produced. Once a demand has been identified and its design mastered, it can be produced more efficiently and more reliably – and hence more cheaply – than ever before.

Consider that other mode of transport – the automobile. When we buy a car we expect it to transport us in comfort to wherever we wish to go.

More than that, we expect someone to build it in the colour we want and with all the options we want. But that is a relatively recent development.

When cars were first invented they were hand-built by engineers and craftspeople. This meant they were very expensive and were the preserve of the wealthy. Then along came Henry Ford. Ford realized that most people had common requirements from a car. This insight allowed him to design a car that could be mass-produced. Ford offered one model only (the Model T) in any colour so long as it was black. But that soon changed as mass-production became more established and car companies, such as General Motors (GM), realized that they could offer more choice and variety at affordable prices. The key to their success lay in identifying common requirements – and common components – across models, which could be produced in large numbers and then assembled.

The road to lean

Recently, the automobile industry has been through another major change, with the advent of the Toyota Production System (TPS). The architect of this is usually acknowledged as being Taichi Ohno, who wrote a short book on the Toyota approach. The TPS was an integral part of Toyota's commitment to quality and people and its roots can be traced back to the 1950s. It came to the world's attention in 1984, when Toyota opened its joint venture with General Motors in California. Then the West woke up and the word began to spread. It was immortalized in the 1990 book, *The Machine that Changed the World*, by James P. Womack, Daniel T. Jones and Daniel Roos,[1] thanks to which the Toyota Production System became known as *lean production*.

In 2007, Toyota's market capitalization was more than one and a half times that of GM, Ford and DaimlerChrysler combined.[2] Headquartered in Japan and employing 285,977 people around the world, Toyota's revenue exceeds US$200 billion. Everyone who follows stories of industrial transformation now knows about Toyota, as its influence extends well beyond the automotive industry.

In recent years, how we think about cars has been transformed by lean thinking in manufacturing. Henry Ford's original idea was to produce a car for 'everyday wear and tear', suitable for the masses. Move on 60 years and not much had changed. If you bought your first car in the late 1960s, you did so when the industry was plagued with reliability issues. Any number of mechanical issues, from the engine to the brakes, from the lights to the battery, could go wrong, causing the car to break down or fail to start. Choosing a car was as much about deciding which model had the cheapest spare parts and most straightforward engine design, to enable as much self-maintenance as possible, as it was about looks and speed.

Move to the present day, post-lean, and automobile reliability is on a different level. The vast majority of cars now start when required and keep going until asked to stop. They rarely break down. A modern driver's mechanical knowledge need stretch no further than knowing how to top up the oil, check the tyre pressure and change the washer liquid.

The story of the car shows how as consumers our expectations constantly evolve. It is also testament to our ability to standardize, systemize and develop the ways by which products are created and improved over the years.

All over the world, people have similar basic needs for products – whether it be mobile phones, transport, cash or, more fundamentally, food, shelter and clothing. Every day thousands of mobile phones are produced, journeys are made and billions are withdrawn from ATMs. They are reliable, affordable and give us what we want.

But that is not true of many of the services we use. Cars may disappear reassuringly into the distance with minimal maintenance, but the service world can appear trapped in a dusty, laboured, paper-ridden world of disappointment. The phone is ringing but no one is picking it up.

So, why can't we take these services for granted in the same way as cars? Why can't we always be confident about reliability? Why can't service providers always predict costs accurately? And why can't we always respond to change as quickly as we would like?

One reason, of course, is that many services are relatively new. IT services, for example, are often still individually designed. They rely on highly skilled people to produce and operate them. Yet all over the world businesses have the same needs for IT services and systems. They require standard operations like sales order processing, HR and financial planning. It seems odd, then, that businesses cannot yet take such services for granted. We believe the future will be very different. The sort of industrial revolution that transformed manufacturing is coming to services.

Service comes to life

For some time now, people have been talking about how to apply the principles of lean production beyond the shop floor to service organizations as diverse as hospitals, banks and government departments. But many commentators agree that efforts in this area have largely failed to deliver.

Applying lean thinking to services, where the work is usually less repetitive and the outcome less tangible, is not straightforward. The famous business thinker Ted Levitt of Harvard Business School explained why by using the analogy of field versus factory. He demonstrated how manufacturing occurs 'here in the factory' where machines produce uniform goods, while service is delivered 'out there in the field' by people. A different approach is required, one that recognizes the differences between manufacturing to a fixed design and providing a service that is able to adapt to the constantly changing needs of end-users.

As an IT service company and a product manufacturer, Fujitsu's knowledge and experience spans both field and factory. Combining these elements has enabled us to come up with the concept of living service. In the words of Daniel Jones, Chairman of the Lean Enterprise Academy, and co-author of *The Machine that Changed the World*, 'Fujitsu has pioneered the field in lean thinking in the service industry and its innovative approach is driving a different way of working and thinking across the organization – and its customers'.[3] In our view, lean thinking is also a part of the living service approach. This approach to service is already delivering benefits to Fujitsu as well as its customers and their customers.

Let us illustrate this point by describing Fujitsu's ongoing journey of delivering service to Toyota. Toyota's success is based on the philosophy of providing 'the right car, in the right place, at the right time',[4] together with a people-focused approach in all areas of its business. In this way, Toyota delivers happiness to its customers. In fact, customer happiness is the main product of Toyota's holistic approach. To deliver such happiness, people across Toyota and around its business ecosystem – both partners and suppliers – continually contribute to the company's efficiency and growth.

In a service context, our focus at Fujitsu is on understanding, honouring and responding to the strategies, processes, technologies, people and cultures of all our customers, including Toyota. Fujitsu's people – led by the head of the automotive industry business, Hiroshi Suyama – strive to understand the Toyota way of doing business and then continually adapt and evolve to help Toyota deliver happiness to its customers.

The relationship between Toyota and Fujitsu dates back more than 40 years. During the early stages of relationship building, Fujitsu's straight talking and tenacious efforts impressed people across Toyota. This helped build trust and multi-level relationships between both companies. In the late 1990s, by working closely with Toyota, Fujitsu designed and deployed a Global Supply Chain Management (G-SCM) system, a streamlined process vital to the Toyota Production, Supply & Logistics System.

Delivery of such service requires alignment to a customer's strategy, processes, technology, people and culture. We use the metaphor of Mind (strategy), Body (processes and technology) and Soul (people and culture) to reflect the organic nature of living service and the richer alignment it creates. To deliver living service, service providers need to understand, honour and respond to the Mind, Body and Soul of their customers throughout their journey together.

Like a lot of great ideas it sounds obvious. So, if living service is so simple why isn't everyone doing it? We think that one day everyone will. But right now we think that Fujitsu is pioneering this living service approach. Think back to when the first Japanese cars started to be imported into the USA and Western Europe. The idea that you build quality into every component – rather than checking for quality after the car is built – seems obvious now. But, at the time, the thinking behind management ideas such as Total Quality Management was revolutionary. It changed manufacturing forever. We believe the same will be true of living service.

Simply put, living service is a progressive way to sell, solve, deliver and innovate services. In the future, it means we will all be able to take more things for granted – freeing companies to focus on the things that matter the most: building relationships with their customers, improving operational efficiency and growing their businesses. This will be vital because we are living in an increasingly service dominated world. And those services are constantly changing.

At Fujitsu, the journey towards living service excellence is under way. It is already transforming the way the company operates and how it works with customers. We believe it is the way services – all services – will occur in the future. The lessons we have learned are directly applicable to all companies. During the course of this book we hope we can share them, so that you, too, can maximize the potential of service in your business.

Press pause

But before we fast-forward your journey to living service, first press pause. Pause to consider the realities, which make maximizing service so vital.

Take a moment to think about the service you have received today. Think about how many service experiences you have had in the last 24 hours – at the supermarket, the post office, a restaurant, a bar, a garage, a hotel, a taxi, a bus, on the telephone. Think of online purchases and experiences. Think of helplines. Service is inescapable and incredibly important to the quality of our lives.

Now, think of what matters to you when you consider service.

Strangely, when you ask people what they value in terms of service there is almost universal agreement. Whether in an airport or a retail store, at a bank counter, on the line to a customer service centre or in an IT department, service is at its best when the technologies behind it are unobtrusive – when it efficiently delivers exactly what customers want, when they want it. Similarly, in our business dealings, many chief executives and chief information officers have told us that they don't want to see IT, they just want it to work invisibly. People can then focus on enjoying their travel, hassle-free shopping, doing timely transactions, resolving their query, or running their business.

Service is best when you see what it does and you appreciate its benefits – but there is no need to understand exactly how it works. Indeed, what goes on behind the scenes of great service is typically invisible – and better that way. When you turn on your PC, for example, you do so in the firm belief that the document you created last week, or last year for that matter, will still be there. The benefit is clear and the service appreciated. But there is no need to have an in-depth knowledge of how the PC achieves this remarkable feat. The same applies to a myriad of other services. On this people agree. The trouble is that this is often not what they receive. To understand why we are so frequently disappointed is the first step on our journey, but it also requires us to understand how service *could* – and, we believe *should* – be.

Let's start by looking at the characteristics of *living service*, a way of thinking and acting, which helps ensure that our expectations of service are delivered.

Service is about people

A colleague told us a story about an experience in Japan. Needing to send some important documents to China, he called a well-known courier company. The company quickly provided him with an English speaking assistant who proceeded to guide him through the delivery process. While on the call, the assistant also filled in all the applicable customs and delivery forms for our colleague. Then, just twenty minutes later, the person from the courier company arrived with the completed customs and delivery forms to collect the documents. The courier noticed that the envelope our colleague was going to use might not be strong enough to protect his important documents, so he offered to go to his van to find something more suitable. He came back with a stronger envelope and helped our colleague pack the documents safely. He also checked all the necessary forms for our colleague. Then, before leaving, the courier provided him with a tracking number and explained to him that he could use this number at the company's website to keep track of where his documents were. Our colleague didn't quite understand the process, so the courier asked to use his laptop to log into the company's website. The courier demonstrated how to use the tracking number to follow the progress of the documents. He then passed the laptop to our colleague, so he could try using the tracking number himself. Satisfied that his customer was able to use the tracking number successfully, the courier offered to save the website under his internet favourites to allow him quick and simple access to it. The courier also ensured that our colleague would be notified by an e-mail once the document had arrived. This saved him from having to track it himself. Indeed, a couple of days later, his contact – to whom he was sending the documents – phoned him to confirm receipt just after he had received an e-mail from the courier.

> First and always, service is about people. Living service is resolutely and inspirationally about maximizing the power of people to provide customers with great experiences.

... and optimized by technology and processes

But, increasingly, service is not just about people: it is also about the technology and how that is supported. The assistant at the courier firm provided a friendly and efficient human face, but relied on technology and pre-programmed processes to track and deliver the package.

Here is another example. One of our constantly travelling colleagues checked into a Chicago hotel. This was her first stay so she was completely unknown to the staff at the hotel. After a few busy days, she checked out and returned to Europe. After her trip she then noticed that she had mislaid her expensive fountain pen. She did not know where she had lost it and so did not make any enquiries – just assumed it was lost. Two years later she returned to Chicago and checked in to the same hotel. To her surprise and delight, on checking in, the receptionist provided her with her pen – she had left it in her room two years before. Despite not having a forwarding address, the staff at the hotel had diligently recorded the loss in the hotel computer system which then flagged up the fact when she checked back in. Technology enabled the hotel receptionist to provide remarkable and personal service.

> Service is increasingly a story of people, technology and processes working together. Living service uses the appropriate technology to help deliver personal, cost-effective and reliable service.

Getting the balance right

There was a time, before modern technology was employed, when service was the human part of commerce. Good service was taken for granted as part of buying any product.

In the industrialized world, as organizations grew and became more competitive, margins reduced and wages increased, so that companies saw the people content of service as a cost overhead to be driven down. Services became seen as a price-competitive commodity. Businesses increasingly used technology and standardization, producing a cheaper but increasingly mechanized service. While appropriate for some services, there were some settings where this mechanized approach failed to satisfy or even recognize people's individual needs.

Let's take, for example, the overuse of automated telephone systems. You have to navigate through a series of multiple choice menus before speaking to someone in a call centre. (If you know the sort we mean, press one; and if you find them helpful, press two!) List after list of menus are provided so that you can choose the service you want (assuming that one is appropriate) before finally you are put in a queue and wait to be connected. After minutes of waiting, despite the patronizing assurance that the call is extremely important to the company (and the ample evidence to the contrary), the phone is answered by someone who is able only to log the call rather than actually do anything to resolve the customer's issue. Such service, though useful from a company perspective, either leaves the customer cold – or hot under the collar. It is not something that has been designed to be people-centric or evolve with modern lifestyles. Indeed, rarely has a so-called service improvement been so universally loathed. Why is this?

John Patrick, one of the pioneers of the internet, had this to say:

Technology has definitely increased the ability for e-businesses to offer world class customer service but unfortunately I believe that the gap between what people expect and what they get is growing. There are some great web sites out there but there are also many that have taken their old processes and attitudes and moved them to the web. Organizations of all kinds have to think about what it means to be open. The words 9–5 M–F mean nothing to teenagers and yet they soon will be an even bigger force in the marketplace – as employees and consumers – than they already are. Call centres are another example of the need to change. People are quite tired of hearing 'please pay attention because our menus have changed'. How could it be that all menus in the world have recently changed? The bottom line is integration. Organizations need to integrate their islands of automation so that they can meet the rapidly rising expectations of their customers. [5]

Overusing technology, while failing to understand or prioritize on the customers' experiences, produces dying service – which drives away customers.

Service calling

The call centre provides a useful example of how over-mechanized dying – as opposed to living – service can result from the rigid application of technology. However, it also demonstrates how living service can produce a totally different experience for the caller.

With a traditional call centre, the experience for the customer is impersonal and often inexpert. Problem calls are received, and the service organization merely manages the flow of that call as it wends its way along the virtual corridors of the organization. Success in such an environment is typically measured by the efficient management of the call (call duration, number of rings to answer and so on) and not by whether the customer's problem has been resolved.

But, in many cases, by empowering the person on the end of the phone customers' problems can be more easily solved. By giving people the tools and capabilities they need to understand what is important to the customer, and identifying patterns of behaviours and recurring problems, living service can be provided.

We encountered a good example of this a few years ago at an international airline. Instead of asking staff at its IT call centre simply to log calls, the airline empowered staff to make the company's service delivery processes transparent so they could analyze the root cause of the calls. It quickly became clear that a disproportionate number of them stemmed from the airline's printers not working. Yes, you heard us correctly: printers not working. In many cases, this was causing lengthy delays at check-in. Working with us, the airline successfully diagnosed and solved a number of these problems, reducing costs and improving the efficiency of its business.

By making such issues transparent to the customer and eliminating the root cause of those problems – often something as comparatively minor as malfunctioning printers – you can provide a more effective response to customers. This is a virtuous circle of continuous innovation – leading to service that adapts and evolves to customers' needs.

By making technology and processes, as well as the capabilities of people transparent, a greater level of service can be provided. Technology is better utilized and there is changing awareness among people as the gap between customer and service provider melts away.

Invisible excellence

This balance between the people and the technology and process sides of service is something with which we have both become fascinated. We refer to these two sides as the art (people) and science (technology and process) dimensions of service. Striking the right balance between them is central to our business, but it is also something more profound because, in one form or another, it touches all of our lives.

When people, technology and processes work together the results are remarkable – though we sometimes take them for granted. No matter how amazing they are, over time we get used to them. As we have said, the remarkable becomes the mundane, but the mundane can also be blissfully and reassuringly reliable.

Imagine this. You are going to Tokyo for a business meeting. From your London home, you call your local taxi company. As you have used the company previously, it has your name and address instantly on its system when you call on your mobile. Minutes later, you are whisked through the early morning London traffic to Heathrow airport. The taxi driver's cab is fitted with the latest SatNav device allowing London's many traffic black spots to be circumvented. Arriving at Heathrow, you check in straight-away. You have already pre-booked your usual seat in the plane (by the window, next to the emergency door for extra legroom) and paid a little extra by clicking the carbon offset button. In the airport you go directly to get some money from an ATM. You then go through the security and passport formalities before arriving at the gate to wait a short time before boarding. Once boarded and airborne, you are provided with a drink and then your chosen lunch from the menu.

Twelve hours later, you arrive in Tokyo. Going through the airport for-malities again you also change money at the currency exchange desk. You then get on the airport limousine bus, which takes you directly to the Conrad Hotel in central Tokyo. There you check in and go to your room. While freshening up, the concierge service presses your suit, which has become wrinkled on the plane. You then take the metro and arrive at your business destination to attend the meeting. Following the meeting, you are taken out for dinner at a nearby restaurant. After dinner, you return to the hotel, check your email and call your family in London before going to bed.

We admit that a story where everything works can be dull. Any number of things could have gone wrong with the day, but did not. The taxi might not have turned up or got stuck on London's North Circular ring road. You might not have got the seat you wanted on the plane or, worse still, the flight may have been delayed until the next day. The currency exchange stand in Tokyo might have been out of money or perhaps the hotel email did not work. Instead, the taxi arrived promptly and got you to the airport, the airline suffered no delays, and the currency exchange had sufficient cash. In all cases, the services required were diligently provided and you got to your meeting on time – and at the end of the day managed to pick up your email and call home.

Also invisible in the shadows was the part technology played in all the services. The SatNav worked in the taxi; the ATM spat out the required amount of money; the airline booking system provided the seat you wanted; the currency exchange stand logged in to the day's exchange rates; the email synchronized; and the telephone connected you with your family. And, in truth, you would never have given any of it a second thought. To you, the people, technology and processes behind the service had become invisible – part of the furniture.

> When routine services work well, people, technology and processes work together; invisible excellence is delivered.

Remarkably simple and elegant

While most of the time we may be happy with this smooth, invisible excellence, there are times when we appreciate the remarkable: when someone quietly notices our individual circumstances and does something extra to help (returning the pen to the hotel guest, for example); when we are stuck in a difficult situation, and somebody goes that extra mile to help us out. That is exactly what happened to a colleague of ours recently.

His wife had caught a bad cold on their holiday in Japan. On their return flight, with Virgin Atlantic, as the plane started its descent into Heathrow, she suddenly got a sharp pain across her forehead. The pain moved from the centre down to her left temple. Needless to say she was in some distress and our colleague was full of concern.

When alerted, an air hostess quickly came to help out. She diagnosed the situation – the passenger's sinuses had become blocked thanks to the cold and the change in cabin pressure as the plane descended. She and three colleagues searched around and quickly produced some menthol smelling tissues to open up the sinuses, a warm towel to reduce the pressure on the forehead and some drinking water to help equalize the pressure. They also coordinated with the ground crew so that when our colleague and his wife disembarked someone was waiting in the terminal to carry their baggage through to passport control. They also arranged for a doctor and a wheelchair to be on hand if necessary. All this was done when they were just 20 minutes from landing.

Our colleague was understandably very impressed, as were we when he told us – and now you are probably impressed, too. This is what happens with great service. People tell their friends and colleagues. Word spreads.

So what can we learn from this? The cabin crew worked together as a team to bring relief and diagnosis as quickly as possible. They did not duplicate anything but helped out in an unobtrusive and efficient manner. This was particularly impressive as the plane was about to land and so they had a lot of other things to do as well.

They also collaborated with others in different parts of the airline. The cabin crew contacted the medical centre and the ground crew to provide a coordinated response to ensure that our colleague's wife would be alright. The senior cabin crew had some medical expertise and took command of the situation. One of the crew sat with the distressed passenger, and provided reassurance and diagnosis. She also helped coordinate the other crew to ensure they brought relief – water and menthol. All the crew had a positive can-do attitude to help. The crew made sure our colleague's wife was 100 per cent recovered before leaving them. The pain subsided as they returned to terra firma, so it was not a major issue.

This great service experience occurred because the cabin crew adapted their behaviour to the situation – they put the person at the centre of the service. Other examples of great service occur because they take place in a field where bad service is the norm. An airport counter with no queue! A coffee machine with drinks that taste really good!

The interesting point is that such examples of great service are not high-tech – or expensive. In fact, they have an elegant simplicity: reassure the passenger and treat her headache; have enough people on duty to avoid queues; provide decent coffee. People loom large in such service stories: they make the difference. (Of course, the cabin crew were able to talk to the medical centre only because of the technology, but that is taken for granted today.) And these are the service experiences that we cherish and remember with pleasure. They are not complicated; in fact, that is a part of their appeal. Think of Picasso being able to draw a bird with a single stroke of his brush or of Miles Davis cutting through the air with a beautiful note on his trumpet. Living service can be breathtakingly simple, so much so that you cannot believe that others have not tried it before.

Great service is remembered and talked about. So as well as making people happy, it also enhances the service provider's reputation and gives them loyal customers. Living service has an elegant simplicity.

Great service adapts and evolves

First and always, service is about people. Now, it is increasingly a story of people, technology and processes working together. Art and science. Service is best when it is built to deliver elegant simplicity and invisible excellence through continuous innovation.

There is one other element. No company can afford to see itself as simply producing products or providing a certain style or standard of service. Those that do are like a machine designed for a static world. Today's organizations must be more organic. And so the final element of living service is that it must enable companies to evolve with their markets by responding to stimuli. Like a plant that grows towards the sun, successful companies respond to changing customer demands. Service should never be static; it must adapt and evolve to fit customers' needs.

Individual and societal aspirations are fluid and ever-changing, so the service you provide must change too. Service is people-centred. Always. This is the essence of living service; it adapts and keeps pace with changing customer demands. It remains in step with the people it is meant to serve. It does not become a slave to processes and systems that will inevitably become obsolete over time.

An example of an industry where we can see such evolutionary change is credit cards. When credit cards were initially introduced they could be used only in the home country of the card issuer. As few people travelled regularly, the cards satisfied customer demand. Indeed, if people did venture abroad then traveller's cheques could fill the gap when taking cash was not appropriate. But, as time wore on, more and more people started to travel. So the credit card evolved. It is now possible to use most cards in most ATMs and many restaurants around the world. Additional services, such as travel and accident insurance, are also provided as part of the credit card service offering, giving further peace of mind to customers. As fraud became another concern for customers, credit card issuers responded by introducing cards with holograms and then cards that required PIN authentication; currently in development are biometric measures to reduce fraud still further. Cards have also launched reward points and affinity schemes. Each time you spend, rewards – either as cash, air miles, hotel points or discounts at your favourite shops – are given to you or, if you are feeling benevolent, to your selected charity or even the sports team you support. Some of these developments, such as international use and fraud prevention measures, were led by customer demand, but others such as insurances, affinity and reward schemes are more proactive in creating better services that people see value in using. Together these can be seen as a living service, staying in touch with customers and enhancing the opportunities and value available to them, while at the same time providing additional revenues to the suppliers.

Living service allows people, technology and processes to adapt and evolve to the changing needs of customers.

The rise of service

Picture the scene. It is a cold day in autumn. You are reading your favourite book as the sun is dipping towards the horizon. It is beginning to go dark as the light in the room ebbs away. Your eyes are beginning to strain while reading the book. What do you do?

For anyone sitting in the developed world, this is of course a stupid question. The answer is that you switch on the light and carry on reading. That's all there is to it.

Our homes have been set up so that our basic needs are catered for. As such, homes today generally all have electricity for light, gas for warmth and water made available. The sources of these products and the companies which supply them vary greatly around the world. The electricity might be generated from coal, nuclear power or a wind turbine. The company supplying it might be municipally run or else a multinational private enterprise. No matter what the case, the essential service we are supplied with remains the same. If we need light, we flick a switch; if we need gas, we turn a knob; if we need water, we turn on a tap.

The services provided here epitomize aspects of living service. They are people-focused: clearly they have been designed and operate to meet the needs of the people they serve. They are built to deliver elegant simplicity and invisible excellence – the pipes and cables which support these services are generally unobtrusive, being behind the cupboards in our homes and under the tarmac of our streets.

The services also continually evolve. Many remote areas around the world, which were previously no-go areas for the supply of water and electricity, for instance, have now been linked to the grid. The services are also highly adaptive. Utility companies, for example, know and anticipate when spikes in demand are likely to occur. Famously in the UK, for instance, they know to expect that millions of people will boil their kettles to make a cup of tea at half-time during an important soccer match, such as the FA Cup Final. And finally, they are enabled by people, technology and processes.

As society evolves, services continually adapt and evolve to keep up. With electricity, for example, environmental concern is leading to a greater proportion of electricity coming from renewable sources rather than fossil fuels.

The basic service – the ability to flick the switch – continues, but the way that service is created continues to evolve in parallel with the needs and concerns of customers.

The sweet smell of service

But we have not always been able to take such services for granted. Take water for instance. In the early nineteenth century, sewage in London flowed from unsealed cesspits through open sewers to the River Thames. The resulting pollution meant that the Thames was devoid of any fish or other wildlife, and an obvious health hazard to Londoners. As a result, cholera epidemics – cholera is spread via contaminated water – struck London with horrific frequency. In 1853 to 1854 more than 10,000 Londoners died from the disease. Then, in 1858, the summer was unusually hot. The Thames and many of its urban tributaries were overflowing with sewage. The warm weather encouraged bacteria to thrive and the resulting smell was overwhelming.

The Great Stink finally prompted parliament into action. A bill was passed and an engineer by the name of Joseph Bazalgette was put in charge of the project. Bazalgette's solution was to construct 83 miles of underground brick main sewers to intercept sewage outflows, and 1,100 miles of street sewers to intercept the raw sewage which until then had flowed freely through the streets and thoroughfares of London. The out-flows were diverted downstream where they were dumped into the Thames. Sewage treatment facilities came several decades later.

Bazalgette's foresight may be seen in the diameter of the sewers. When planning the network he took the densest population, gave every person the most generous allowance of sewage production and came up with a diameter of pipe needed. He then said, 'Well, we're only going to do this once and there's always the unforeseen', and doubled the diameter to be used. Every Londoner should be grateful for this foresight: the unforeseen was the tower block. If he had used his original, smaller pipe diameter the sewers would have overflowed in the 1960s. So successfully did Bazalgette create the future, the sewers are still in use to this day.

The effect of the new sewer system was to reduce cholera. The city no longer carried an unforgettable odour and water supplies ceased to be cont-aminated by sewage. Today, the Thames contains several smaller varieties of fish, including trout; it is also safe to swim in – for those brave enough.

The direct result is a sewage system which has become a vital service for London. People-focused, elegantly simple, seamlessly invisible, adap-tive and enabled by people, technology and processes – it contains all the elements required to provide us with that most basic of services. What is important to Londoners is not the engineering achievement, but that they can flush their toilets hygienically, efficiently and unobtrusively.

When service goes badly wrong, however, we really notice it. A delayed plane; being ignored in a shop when wanting to purchase something; auto-mated answering machines at call centres or an ATM that is out of cash: that's what we notice – and what we tell our friends and family about.

Why does this matter? Well, whether you are a peripatetic executive travelling the world on business, a daily commuter, a home-worker or a retiree, service is a key part of our day-to-day lives. Service is not only per-sonal, it is also commercial. Service can make or break companies. No one would do business with a logistics business that failed to deliver parcels and no one would do business (not for long anyway) with an IT company whose equipment kept breaking down. Harvard's Ted Levitt put it like this: 'There are no such things as service industries. There are only indus-tries whose service components are greater or less than those of other industries. Everybody is in service.'[6]

Levitt's point has never been more true. When it goes well, service can be efficiently unobtrusive – as in the example of the London to Tokyo traveller – and potentially a source of positive pleasure – like the attentive personal service of the cabin crew on the descent into Heathrow. But if it goes wrong, as Bazalgette would tell you, there is always a stink.

> A great service is one that we take for granted and do not need to think about – it has become (sometimes literally) part of the furniture. We only notice it when something goes wrong.

The choice challenge

Everyone is in service, as Ted Levitt stated. For companies, differentiating themselves from the crowd has never been more important or difficult.

Today, consumers have more product and service choice than ever before. In the advanced nations of the world, prosperity, the globalization of trade and increased leisure time have all played their part in providing people with an astonishing array of products. You can buy summer fruits in the depths of winter, rare first editions from bookshops on the other side of the world, or sea food which was caught thousands of miles away only hours ago.

Within the context of greater choice, there is an ongoing debate regarding ownership versus access to service. If the service you require is suitably reliable, affordable, adaptable and elegantly simple and you can access it on demand, there is no need for you to own the service yourself. You may think, for example, that you need to *own* a car. Actually, your real need is for transportation from, for instance, your home to your office and if you could access a service to satisfy that need your requirement for ownership would diminish. Another way of looking at it is to think about why you should own a number of music CDs when you could access a download service at any time. As we have discovered, living service is, among other things, elegantly simple and evolves with the customer's needs. It changes the way people understand and then use service. As a result, service providers need continually to adapt and evolve their services to match changing demand.

Moreover, such choice is available via an increasing range of channels. Think about it. Not so long ago the only place you could exercise your musical taste was in a record shop. If you lived in a small town with limited transport links there might be only one record shop available to you. Whether you could buy the record you actually wanted depended on what was in stock and that often depended on the eclectic tastes of the owner. Nowadays, large music chains are numerous in all our major towns and cities. If one music shop does not have what you want, you can always go to the next shop or ask them to order it for you. Or you might decide not to leave your house at all and order your music online from a website. Or you might decide just to stream it when you want it.

Choice abounds in terms of products, services and channels. From being able to buy music from only one shop between the hours of 9 am and 5 pm, Monday to Friday, you can now purchase any album 24 hours a day either in a physical shop or online.

And yet, despite the proliferation of product choice, there has not always been a corresponding increase in service. To take our music example a little further, imagine that your 'old time' neighbourhood record shop was noted for its owner's forthright opinions on the latest musical trends. For a customer wanting to have a new album recommended to them, the owner provided an invaluable service. The owner's in-depth knowledge allowed him to ask the customer the right questions so as to understand their musical likes and dislikes and then to recommend a recent release which would be of interest.

Fast-forward to now, and the national chains of music shops. In order to keep costs down (something it has to do to compete with online rivals), the shop has reduced staff numbers to a minimum. The job requirements have also changed. It employs staff on the basis of whether they can work the cash till rather than have any particular liking or knowledge of the early work of Bruce Springsteen, for example, much less expressing an opinion on the state of music today.

In order to cater to every possible market, the shop sells a hundred times more albums than the old shop did. No longer will your choices be guided by the recommendations of a trusted adviser – now you can choose from everything. Choice has increased, but so has the complexity of choosing.

The increase in product availability and the advantages inherent with that are not in dispute. But what about service? Product ubiquity does not satisfy everyone's basic service requirements – you want someone to recommend which album you should buy: *Darkness on the Edge of Town* or *Nebraska*? Of course, some people will say that online reviews and recommendations and the like offer an alternative, but it is not the same as the trusty record store owner looking you in the eye and making a personal recommendation.

> Service providers face an ongoing challenge to satisfy customer choice with a commensurate level of service. Moreover, the future challenge will be to provide access to certain services which previously customers would have wanted to own themselves.

No one said it was easy

There is a danger with service in thinking that it is easy. Getting close to customers and so on always sounds straightforward. The invisibility of much of the technology and human resources behind great service is beguiling. We quickly take it for granted that we can take euros out of ATMs in Rome from our bank account in London. Service is akin to the serene progress of a swan swimming in a river: on the top it may appear calm and unflappable, while a few inches beneath the waterline it is paddling furiously.

Indeed, the visible part of a service may be very small in comparison to what is going on in the background. Well-honed service can take years to perfect. In fact, in any industry, product development comes first and overall service tends to lag behind.

We work in the IT industry, which is plagued with the sort of service issues and reputation problems that the automobile industry suffered from 40 years ago. How many times have new software applications come to market with bugs in them? This simply reflects the extremely complex nature of software programming.

We should not be surprised by this, perhaps. After all, as we have noted, the IT industry is relatively young, whereas cars have now been around for over 100 years.

During this period cars have changed – but not nearly as much. It is true that new features such as SatNav (really an IT innovation) now come as standard on some models, but the familiar platform of four wheels, internal combustion engine and braking mechanisms remains. The fact is, too, that what the car does has not altered a great deal since it was invented. It remains a convenient form of transport. In the IT area, technology is advancing at great speed. While IT is progressing via ever-greater product innovation, the automobile industry has spent much more effort on improving the overall service of the car. Cars are now more reliable and environmentally sustainable than before; IT has just become more complicated!

Despite the added complexity in this instance, technology exists to make life more convenient. Whether it is through automating a process, like the ATM in the airport, speeding up a transaction, like the currency exchange stand, or making a new service possible, like allowing the seats on a plane to be reserved, the underlying principle of any technology service (as with any other service) is that it should make life easier for its customers. That is all well and good. But, as we all know, it doesn't always work like that.

> Service succeeds when it provides invisible excellence. When a technology's inherent complexity impacts on the benefits it should provide to the customer, then it has failed.

The whole of the iceberg

While technological issues can be overcome, dealing with people in order to provide great service can be even more daunting. How does a service provider know what their customer really needs? How can the provider ensure that the proffered service is the ideal one?

Traditionally a customer may state a problem and then leave it to the service provider to come up with a solution. Such stilted interaction leaves room for error. How the customer describes a problem and how the service provider then interprets the problem could differ. Moreover the problem is compounded, as often the customer may not know what they really need. How could they? What they say and how they describe the solution may add elements of personal bias into an already intractable problem.

It is, moreover, a fact that 'words may express only 10 per cent of the image a customer has in mind'.[7] The vast majority of our knowledge – the underwater part of the iceberg, so to speak – is captured and shared tacitly through direct interaction among people. By tacit we mean experience-based knowledge, which cannot be easily expressed in words or numbers. Such experiences are hugely important to our personalities. And as companies are made up of people, so tacit knowledge is also important at an organizational level. It is only by really appreciating the tacit knowledge of our customers that we can truly provide great service for them.

> Through its focus on people and the long term, living service leverages tacit knowledge. It does so by understanding, honouring and responding to the Mind, Body and Soul of the customer, the explicit science and the tacit art.

Towards living service

The examples we have looked at highlight some important questions. What is great service today? How can you ensure it keeps pace with customer expectations in the future? We have looked at the characteristics of living service at its best. The rest of this book explains Fujitsu's continuing journey towards living service excellence, and how other organizations can also transform themselves to deliver the service of the future – living service – today. We have chosen examples from a wide range of services, from utilities to media, from transport to retail, that all of us encounter in our daily lives. Figure 0.1 illustrates how we use a myriad of services every day and usually take them for granted – unless, of course, something goes wrong!

Living service continually adapts and evolves to customers' needs. To deliver living service, service providers need to consider three major elements: *Mind, Body and Soul* (see Figure 0.2). We use the metaphor of Mind, Body and Soul to reflect the organic nature of living service, and the powerful combination of theory, practice and inspiration that supports it.

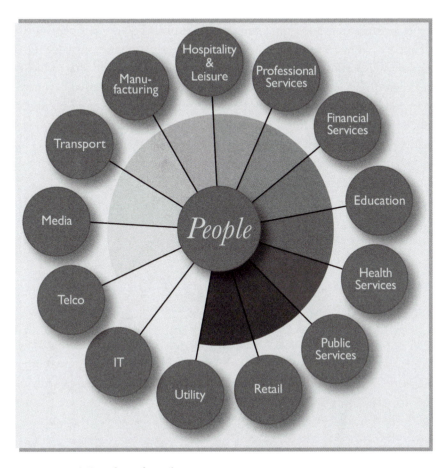

FIGURE 0.1 ◆ **People and services**

In Part 1 of the book, we focus on the *Mind*. The Mind is what makes everything work and is the function that sets direction and develops strategy. The part consists of two chapters. First is the development of a living service culture. It is a philosophy that, together with empowering people, drives service transformation. This section, using real examples, explains how to create a service culture around customer needs.

Then we look at the ways of changing the game by doing things differently and focusing on previously unrecognized customer needs. This can enable you to create new markets and, probably, make the existing competition irrelevant, leading to true competitive advantage.

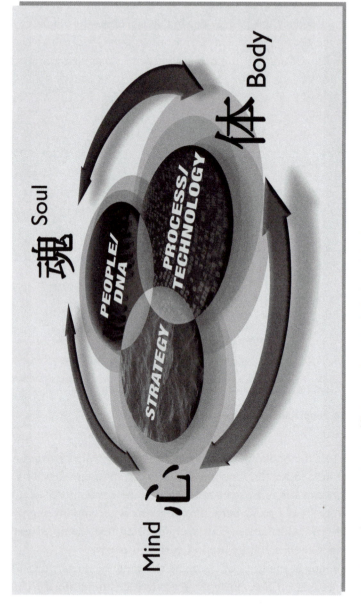

FIGURE 0.2 ◆ Key constructs of living service: Mind, Body and Soul

The Mind seeks to capture the strategic alignment between the service provider, customer and potentially the customer's customer. For a meeting of minds, a sharing of both the tacit and explicit elements needs to be in place. We shall explain how you do this in the 'Changing the Game' chapter.

Part 2 is the *Body* element. The Body consists of processes and technology within an organization. It is the physical structure that changes in context with the evolving needs of the customer. Companies that master living service transform themselves to align with customers' needs: this enables both to grow their businesses. In our view, the Body provides a channel for energy to flow from the Soul (people) throughout the organization.

The Body is built around our interconnected Four Row Model – sell, solve, deliver, innovate. By taking out complexity, enabling customers to choose the right solution to meet their needs now and in the future, and efficiently deploying the services, living service takes selling services to another level.

Selling services is one thing; delivering them – as every customer knows – is another matter entirely. Robust and reliable services that can adapt and evolve are vital to meet the rapidly changing business needs of customers and are at the heart of living service. Consistent and exacting standards are built in.

One of the failings of traditional service offerings is the inability to adapt to future trends. Worse, sometimes customers discover they are not protected from predictable changes in technology. Living service confronts this issue head on. The service provider and customer work together to anticipate change. Often this involves helping customers understand the likely impact of future shocks. Continued future growth depends on trust – which means that a realistic understanding of future technology and business trends needs to be considered. Again, we use some examples to illustrate these points.

The final part of the living service triad is *Soul*. The Soul is the inner essence or energy that keeps the Mind and Body together. To design, build and deliver living service, it is vital to harness the collective energy of people and also leverage the culture (or DNA) embedded within organizations.

Finally, we consider the longer-term social, economic and environmental imperatives for sustaining service. Living service after all does not exist in a vacuum. Think back to the story of London's sewers and our usage of gas, electricity and water. From a pure passive receipt of service perspective, it is difficult to see how things could improve further. And yet, despite this, evolution is continuing. For many of us, it is no longer enough to be satisfied that we are receiving electricity; it is increasingly important that electricity should be clean, green and sustainable. Whether it be by technological innovation, consumer demand or new regulation, utilities – just like any other service – will need to address the issue of sustainability. We believe that the journey towards living service excellence will make services progressively more sustainable in the years to come.

In summary

To summarize what we have learned so far, living service is:

♦ Focused on serving people. It is communicated, designed and operated to meet the needs of the people it serves.

♦ Enabled by people and optimized processes/technologies. As society evolves, methods for interacting with customers also change. Service needs continually to adapt and evolve to keep up.

♦ Transparent. Transparency means openness to show the processes/technologies for continued innovation in the field.

♦ Built to deliver invisible excellence and elegant simplicity through continuous innovation.

♦ Adaptive. It evolves to provide the required flexibility to co-create the future.

Living service is a combination of art and science that leverages knowledge and experience. It adapts and evolves to customers' needs. To deliver living service, service providers need to understand, honour and respond to the Mind, Body and Soul of customers and their customers, and look at the entire service journey.

In this book, as well as introducing Fujitsu's continuing journey towards living service excellence, we provide pointers for an agenda to show how others can also transform themselves. Initially we need to set a direction, and develop a service culture and a strategy (the Mind); then engage the organization, strengthen our technological and process capabilities through connecting the dots (the Body); and finally maximize energy for the whole organization (the Soul) to make it happen. This transformation journey is distilled in these headline living service agenda items which we will elaborate throughout the book:

- Agenda 1 – Develop a Living Service Culture
- Agenda 2 – Change the Game
- Agenda 3 – Engage with Customers
- Agenda 4 – Accelerate Customers' Opportunities
- Agenda 5 – Deliver Great Service
- Agenda 6 – Co-create the Future
- Agenda 7 – Maximize Collective Energy

PART 1

Mind 心 Kokoro

In humans, the mind orchestrates our actions. It is the control centre, where we analyze situations and make decisions. The same is true in our model of living service.

The Mind is what makes everything work. It is the function that sets direction and develops strategy. It identifies what is important for the organization, and for everyone in the organization.

Just as with human beings, it is inextricably linked with both the Body and the Soul. The Mind controls the synthesis of people, technology and processes which makes up living service.

The Mind part is divided into two:

Developing a Living Service Culture: Chapter 1 shows how to create a culture where everything you do is done around customers and their customers.

Changing the Game: Chapter 2 builds on this by explaining how the very nature of service is changing and how you can do things differently rather than doing business in the traditional way.

CHAPTER 1

Developing a Living Service Culture

et's start with what we call a *service mindset*. Imagine this: your 15-year-old daughter has exams coming up. She has been working hard throughout the school year, but a few weeks ago a bout of tonsillitis meant that she missed a number of classes and she is now struggling to catch up. As the exam dates loom ever closer, the extra stress this creates makes it even more difficult for her to grasp the missing knowledge she needs. She has told the teachers of her difficulties, but they have been instructed that they must continue to follow the syllabus during timetabled class time, to ensure that all the examination areas are covered by the end of the academic year. Then one day she comes home and tells you that some of her teachers have decided to run extra classes after school hours for a group of pupils who were experiencing similar difficulties. Immediately she has relaxed as she feels she will now get the help she needs and within a few weeks she is back to her old confident self.

The teachers did not have to supply the extra classes; they were under no obligation and could simply watch their students struggle on. Why did they do it? Because they understood that the value of the service they provide lies in *educating* their students, not in merely delivering a syllabus to a timetable, and because they cared about this. Taking a broader view of the service you are providing – having a service mindset – is a central ingredient of a living service culture.

It is worth returning to the observations of Harvard's Ted Levitt.[1] Levitt argued that the central preoccupation of corporations should be with satisfying customers rather than simply producing goods. He said, 'management must think of itself not as producing products but as providing customer-creating value satisfactions'. Levitt observed that production-led thinking inevitably led to narrow perspectives. He argued that companies must broaden their view of the nature of their business, just as the teachers did when they provided extra classes. Otherwise their customers, such as the pupils, will soon be forgotten.

In a similar vein, Levitt wrote:

> *The railroads are in trouble today not because the need was filled by others … but because it was not filled by the railroads themselves. They let others take customers away from them because they assumed themselves to be in the railroad business rather than in the transportation business. The reason they defined their industry wrong was because they were railroad-oriented instead of transportation-oriented; they were product-oriented instead of customer-oriented.*

The railroad business was constrained, in Levitt's view, by a lack of willingness to expand its horizons. Levitt went on to level similar criticisms at other industries. The film industry failed to respond to the growth of television because it regarded itself as being in the business of making movies rather than providing entertainment.

Move forward half a century and Levitt's warnings remain relevant: narrowly define who your customers are and you run the risk of excluding customers; narrowly interpret the service you provide in terms of its delivery mechanisms or features only and you run the risk of losing out to competitors who think of the overall benefit of the service. A teacher, for example, who provides an education rather than delivering a syllabus; a railroad company that provides the overall transportation needs of the customer, not just the railroad element; or a film studio that provides entertainment rather than simply making movies.

Such feature-oriented service is commonplace. How many of us have been frustrated by service providers who do not care about the final value of their service to us, but only about the way they have decided to do things? These suppliers do not have the living service culture we have just discussed. We hope and anticipate that their time is running out.

So, first, let us think about what service culture is and how it can be developed.

Service culture is an environment in which the behaviour of individuals is guided by underlying values that support the delivery of what customers want, where they want it, when they want it and how they want it. It is only by reaching out to understand what the customer really needs that you can offer insightful connections and identify fresh opportunities. Building this understanding requires a deep commitment to improving your customer's situation and the ability to have open and honest conversations. It may take a while for both parties to build a relationship to the point where they can have these conversations but, once they take place, a realistic vision of the future possibilities for both customer and service provider can emerge.

As different organizations serve different customers who want different things, so service culture will have a different look from one organization to another. In creating a living service culture the key element is that everything you do, you must do around customers and their customers. This is the fundamental tenet from which you can set off on your living service journey.

Everything you do, do around customers and their customers

Time is running out for suppliers who think of service only in terms of features. A service provider now needs to consider the whole picture – to understand all the benefits to the customer and their customer that flow from the service.

This can be achieved by creating a customer engagement model based on the delivery of the customers' business value, rather than simply delivering a package of services. Put simply, this is a model that extends your thinking beyond your customers' business to how your customers deliver value to their customers. To do this well, every element of your business – from the initial engagement, through the development of a solution and its delivery, to continual innovation – needs to be fully aligned to your customer. In other words, rather than customer engagement supporting your business model, customer engagement should be at the core of your business model.

An example of this may be seen with a government agency we work with. A key part of its role is to investigate breaches of regulations. A large proportion of its work, especially its high profile activity, involves running specific investigative projects. Over time, the organization became concerned that some of its systems, rather than assisting staff, were beginning to get in the way of them doing their jobs. This was making it difficult for staff to meet the requirements of external customers.

The organization wanted to build an environment where its employees could easily organize themselves around their investigations. This meant using technology to foster more flexible working patterns. For example, it wanted its staff to be able to log in on any computer in the building and be able to access their own unique information and tools to do their work on a particular project. It also wanted them to be able to log in to the telephone system so that phone calls would follow them to wherever they were working. Hot-desking would allow staff to organize themselves around their projects rather than their services, improving flexibility, reducing workload and increasing the speed and quality of work.

Good in theory, but the trouble with flexibility is that it is a difficult thing to create a contract for. Unforeseen challenges arrive and new technologies to meet those challenges become available every few months or even weeks. This means an agreement signed today to deliver an optimum solution could very easily be out of date in a matter of weeks.

The regulator did not want a fixed set of solutions and services or an out-of-the-box solution. It wasn't particularly interested in specific email systems or databases but about outcomes that it really wanted for its business, such as flexible working.

What was amazing, talking to the customer, was that Fujitsu was the only one of the potential suppliers to go back and ask for clarification of what exactly it was looking for. The other potential suppliers already had their solutions at hand – no matter what the client wanted. Fujitsu really wanted to deliver something that was the right fit for the customer, not just what was right for Fujitsu. The more questions you ask, the more answers you will find. As Fujitsu asked questions, what had been a complex set of decisions for the customer began to look ever simpler.

Increasingly the regulator began to appreciate much more precisely what it really wanted and how it could be achieved. Over time, a collaborative picture began to emerge of a future roadmap to transform its business. By transforming itself, a supplier can help engender transformation in its customer too. Such an effect automatically helps strategic alignment between supplier and customer. You are on the same page and conditioned to help each other turn over to the next page.

What was also important to the regulator was having the technology and processes to foster and encourage flexible working – not what particular type of software and hardware it might use. By delving deeply into the customer environment to understand what customers really need, an important step towards living service is taken.

A key element in supporting this collaborative approach is, of course, the expertise and knowledge of your people. For many traditional service providers, only a limited number of people will really be aware of the customer's requirements. Imagine how much more value can be provided if the customer's needs – including tacit elements – are understood by all the people throughout the service provider. When this happens there is an opportunity for real alignment between how the customer and the service provider think.

This is astonishingly rare. Just as people can be self-absorbed (focused inwards), so can organizational structures and processes. If a large number of your employees are mainly concerned with running internal processes or chasing internal targets then you will find it difficult to embed a service culture, and impossible to introduce living service. This is simply because, for a majority of your employees, real external customers are just too far away for them to relate to. The important day-to-day things for them are not looking outwards towards customers, but inwards at their processes.

We have found that such a situation can limit a service provider's chances of truly understanding a customer and so be able successfully to deliver a great service. Part of Fujitsu's transformation journey has been to address this.

Back in 2004, for example, Fujitsu was working with Reuters. Founded in London in 1851, Reuters is best known as the world's largest international multimedia news agency. Yet more than 90 per cent of the company's revenue actually comes from its financial services business. Reuters products are used by 370,000 financial market professionals working in the global equities, fixed income, foreign exchange, money, commodities and energy markets.

Reuters customers are among the most demanding in the world. Traders need access to financial information every second of every day. Even milliseconds of delay in service/information delivery result in lost business for Reuters customers. So Reuters needs all of its service providers to be absolutely in tune, able tenaciously to deliver to the same levels of service as Reuters delivers to its customers. This includes providing great service to Reuters employees around the world. The trouble was that back in 2004 Reuters was unhappy with Fujitsu's service – and Fujitsu was unhappy with the existing Reuters contract.

But in the summer of that year, Bill Simpson became the Fujitsu account manager for Reuters. In his own words, he saw an opportunity to 'transform' the relationship and believed that there was tremendous scope for improvement with the account. Simpson's timing was good. Reuters had a new CEO with a transformation agenda and Fujitsu believed it could add value to his 'Fast Forward' change programme at Reuters. A new CIO, David Lister, joined Reuters in late 2004, with an agenda to drive up service quality, efficiency and consistency around the world and to build better, more open relationships with suppliers in order to do so. Reuters and Fujitsu shared each other's priorities and challenges. The seeds of a relationship were sown. Minds became aligned.

What we learned from working with Reuters is that, in order to embed a service culture, areas traditionally designed or that had evolved without reference to customers needed to be redesigned with the external customer in mind. For many companies the only people tasked and measured by customer measures are external-facing staff, such as sales people, service delivery managers and customer services. These people can be successful only if supported by the rest of the organization. Everyone needs to understand their personal input into the customers' experience, and share in the consequences of it, both good and bad. Job descriptions and performance reviews for all staff should be focused on supplying external customer value.

This appears obvious, but happens all too infrequently. Traditional finance departments, for example, often focus on internal processes. Their limited contact with customers may be to chase up invoices, but their ability to affect the quality of service provision to customers is tremendous. In reality, they often control the timely flow of resources around an organization and may also be required to look at business cases for service evolution, and a host of other activities which directly affect the quality of service an organization can deliver. By not seeing the connection to the customer experience, they might not have the same sense of urgency about these tasks and so slow the speed of service evolution.

Our message is that having understood the customer – and typically the customer's customers too – you must align the provision of your service to their needs and experience. This is why we have emphasized the importance of doing everything around customers and their customers.

Earn the trust of your customers and employees

A service culture requires trust. Treating people with respect will allow you to develop trust with employees who are charged with delivering living service and customers who receive it. It is vital that both groups feel able to have open and honest conversations so that they can share their problems without hesitation. A customer who feels unable to share commercially or politically sensitive information may end up with a service that provides less value than they originally envisaged. The fit of services when they are delivered will not be as good as they could have been if all information had been shared. This creates wasted effort and cost. The service provider should also be able to be just as open with customers. By providing transparency of delivery processes you are increasing a customer's faith in your ability to deliver what you have promised. We share our future roadmaps – a description of expected future developments – for this reason. It is like being able to see a clean cooking area in a restaurant: reassuring.

There is no complex magical theory for garnering respect. Often the most simple things make a difference. Fujitsu delivers IT services to the Transport Accident Commission (TAC), the statutory insurer of third-party personal liability for road accidents in the state of Victoria in Australia. The two teams are co-located in the same building and those in the same project sit next to each other. And to enhance this communication, Paul Bourke, the Fujitsu account director, regularly walks the floors to pick up any issues he can get from the customers. Respect is fostered among people across all layers of the organization. As such, a strong long-term relationship has been built up based on mutual trust and cooperation.

Of course, both customers and providers can be poor at sharing information when they feel that the other party may not have their best interests at heart or that they may risk exposing vulnerabilities that could be taken advantage of. Trust can only be achieved by acting in the interests of employees and customers from the first contact and throughout the relationship.

It must come from the heart. It can take years of demonstrating this relationship to build the trust required – but only minutes to destroy it. Trying to deceive people by telling them how much you value them when you don't believe this will never work. Eventually you will slip up, and they will remember it. In the service business, reputation is everything.

Employees may resist raising customer problems with managers for fear of it reflecting poorly on them. But unless they do so, managers cannot put in the processes to help them and consequently evolve the service. A blame culture, which undermines rather than invigorates collective energy, clearly has no place within a living service.

We have also learned how important cultural and personal celebrations are to people. (Just forget an important birthday in your family and see what happens!) Moments of celebration are a clear demonstration of what is important to a group and provide positive reinforcement of the values and behaviour that are being celebrated.

Most companies celebrate the winning of a major new deal or project. They are saying with these celebrations that winning new business is important to the organization and they appreciate the work that got them there. This is right, of course; winning new business is something to celebrate, but how many people celebrate their customers' successes?

We have found that by ensuring that you celebrate your customers' successes, ideally with your customers, your employees will feel more involved with your customers. This increases their motivation to continue service improvements. At the same time, the celebration reinforces customer service values by declaring explicitly that the customers' end results are the true measure of your success.

Moreover, giving up on customers and their problems sends all kinds of messages to employees – but the big one is that failure is allowed. Imagine what would have happened if, instead of leveraging the Fujitsu culture and ethos, Bill Simpson had given up on the Reuters account in 2004. The lesson? You must tenaciously deliver what customers really need and in doing so demonstrate to everyone in the customer organization that they are the focus of everything you do.

By not doing this you undermine the value of all the other work done in creating a living service and the service culture which supports it. When anyone allows the possibility of failure into their mind their ability to develop solutions is immediately limited. When they refuse to give up, new solutions will always emerge.

Imagine your trip home from work. If your usual route home is blocked by roadworks you will find a way around them. If your usual transport is not available – your car breaks down or your train is cancelled – you will find another way, or walk, but you never give up on your goal to get home. Getting home is not something that you *try* to do – it is something that you *will* do.

This unquestioning conviction to resolve any difficulties no matter what the obstacle is a key element of the service culture that supports living service. It has to be – because living service is about supporting customers who are continually evolving. To support that evolution, the service provider must empower and encourage each individual within it to support any steps necessary which together help provide a living service. Every new problem solved, every difficulty overcome, every extra piece of value delivered is a necessary evolution in order to meet the customers' needs continually. It is only by continuous innovation, after all, that you move closer to your destination.

Put people at the centre of everything

The focus of technology in service is usually all about how fast companies get a cost return on their capital expenditure and the guys behind it aren't thinking warm thoughts about customers. This is one reason why implementation often seems to occur without adequate testing and systems collapse in front of the customer. These hasty implementations with glitches help to give technology a bad name.

So laments Tony Cram of Ashridge Business School and author of *Customers That Count*. He argues that good service has both hard and soft components. On the hard side are elements such as speed, 24-hour convenience, reliability and consistency. 'Technology – when properly specified and tested – can provide these as well or better than a human being', he says. Trouble comes on the softer side of service (the art), which is more intimate and memorable because it involves personal contact.

The soft side is the area of personalization, flexibility and surprise. Humans are generally much better than computers at these aspects. Ideally the technology should be used to provide a standard fast and impersonal service to customers who want to pay a lower cost and who are less valuable to the organization. This frees up employees to give personal service to the customers who deserve or need the individual personalization and flexibility. [2]

Beyond 'doing everything around your customers', and 'earning the trust of your customers and employees' we have learned that it is necessary to put people at the centre of everything.

It is easy to think of instances where we have received great service, when we have been treated as a person rather than a machine. Restaurants where the waiter has engaged with you, given you the benefit of his recommendations for example, are much more memorable than those where no such interactions take place.

In the corporate sphere – on the macro scale – such human touches are also extremely important, and most leading organizations already know this. Consider the case of ASIC (Allianz Shared Infrastructure Services) – the internal IT Infrastructure services supplier of Allianz, one of the top financial institutions in the world, employing over 170,000 people around the globe. A few years ago, in the face of increasing competition and the desire to improve services to customers the company decided to outsource much of its IT operations in Germany.

In the years leading up to the outsourcing decision ASIC had gone through a merger with Dregis, the IT subsidiary of Dresdner Bank (a wholly owned subsidiary of Allianz since 2001), followed by a programme to improve the efficiency of its services. Caring for its employees had always been important to both Allianz and ASIC and they were very concerned that this remained a core value through the changes that were taking place. As an organization it realized that the motivation and trust of its people were very important if a successful restructuring of the operations was to occur, to satisfy its customers and shareholders. If the highest priority was not given to its people, this could damage its service provision and reputation within its most valuable home market.

For ASIC, cost reduction and service improvement from a service provider were not enough. ASIC wanted to make sure that its people were transferred to a company that supported their professional development and provided them with interesting career opportunities. This was just as important as saving money and accessing better and more flexible services. In fact ASIC believed that keeping people happy through the outsourcing was the foundation that would allow further improvements in costs and service to be realized.

The outsourcing agreement meant that over 450 people would transfer their employment from ASIC to the service provider. If the transfer went smoothly and the staff were kept motivated, it could provide ASIC with an excellent opportunity to develop its services to customers. In the worst case, ex-employees not content with the new arrangement, could hold up the benefits – effectively stalling the service improvements promised.

ASIC's COO, Dr Kurt Servatius later commented: 'One of our main criterion in looking for a partner in this field was giving the personnel affected bright prospects for the future.'

ASIC is not the only company looking after the interests and development opportunities for its workforce. For ASIC HR processes and practices were as important as IT process and practices. How it was going to assess the skills of staff, how it would manage the transition and ensure that people were placed into the right jobs, were the big issues.

It bears endless repetition: service is about people. Yet, as service automation spreads throughout the world, people are slowly being pushed out of the service arena. Manned kiosks become self-service vending machines; telephone operators become call routing systems. This is mainly driven by a need to force down costs and offer an any-time service, but organizations should proceed with caution. Technology should enhance the customer experience, not detract from it. Retailers using technology such as the internet or self-service kiosks wisely, can benefit from having multiple sales channels. In marketing-speak, this is about 'leveraging the brand', allowing a company to reach a wider customer base. For the layperson it means using websites, self-service kiosks and other technology to enhance – not replace – personalized interactions: people and technology working in harmony.

Whenever person-to-person interaction is lost, the ability to understand customers is reduced. Without understanding both the tacit and explicit needs of the customer, a living service cannot be provided. Only people can create and sustain the two-way dialogue required to deliver a living service. Their flexibility allows them to respond to nuances and completely individualize a customer interaction. They have the capability to understand what is of real value to customers, rather than just what is in the contract, and so manage unforeseen events in the ways most appropriate for the customer, developing great service for the future.

To provide great service, not only customers of service providers but also employees of those companies need to be energized and happy. The challenge is to ensure that employees can realize their own potential and their customers' dreams. People's emotions do not disappear when they go to work. If you treat your employees and customers with respect, this becomes a norm for the organization and they will treat others with respect, including their colleagues and customers. If you treat your employees poorly you set the benchmark for how your organization values people, and that is the example they will seek to emulate with their colleagues and customers.

Setting the right example is key. Promoting managers who demonstrate a high focus on customers sends a strong message that making customers a priority is important. People should not just be rewarded and promoted on the strength of the profits they bring in from customers, but also on the strength of the relationship with those customers. This sends a clear, often tacit message to others in the company that you get ahead by putting the customer first, developing innovative solutions that focus on delivering real value, and sharing this knowledge cooperatively with your colleagues.

As a consequence, the ability to understand the emotional dimension of communication is invaluable. A complaining customer may not want to do anything other than have their voice heard, or may raise issues in one area because they still have unresolved feelings about an earlier incident in an unrelated area. It takes good people to understand and manage these situations.

Of course, emotion is not just a negative feature for service providers to manage. It has a positive aspect, too. Think of the enjoyable banter of a hairdresser or the reassurance of a doctor – both provide positive emotional outcomes that may be just as important as the advertised service they provide. Would hundreds of thousands cram stadiums each week to watch robot sports or concerts? If they did, it would probably be because of the value of being in a crowd of other people. Simply put, people like meeting and interacting with other people. This in itself has a value over and above the services you are providing. Service providers need to remember this, as they evolve and transform their services.

Empower champions of change

As well as putting people at the centre, we need to add another ingredient: people must have the ability to change things in order to serve their customers better. Only then can they collaborate with their customers without the hidden agenda of fitting the customer to the service. Being prescriptive and inflexible with what people are able to offer as services limits what your customers can get. It also limits what your employees can think about, and so instantly turns a living service into a dying one.

In its product-focused days, Fujitsu provided its account teams with a technical sales information booklet. This encouraged technical discussions to be the focus of initial meetings with customers. It also had the unfortunate effect of narrowing the conversation and limiting the value we could provide to the customer. As our scope of business expanded to include service as well as product solutions, account teams were encouraged to draw on the entire resources of the company to offer services ranging from business process consulting and transformation to IT solutions and managed services. The conversations Fujitsu now has are broad in their scope. Many different paths now exist for the delivery of value to any customer, in any situation. To investigate these options takes a much greater understanding of the customer's needs, but the extra value delivered in both the short and long term makes it more than worthwhile. The proposed solutions will often still bring in a host of technologies, but the technologies are not the discussion point: the customer and their business requirements are.

A service culture means that instead of working to narrow functional objectives, people give priority to the customer and the customer's business objectives. Instead of simply fixing IT or indeed any business function which may not be performing, such as finance, logistics or sales – which are often symptoms of failings elsewhere – staff are empowered and encouraged to work together in finding and fixing the root causes of those problems so that they do not happen again. The answer lies in the way people are guided to approach customer problems and the way they work together.

Imagine you go into a shop to buy a new washing machine. By browsing and chatting with the shop assistant you find the model you want. When you are paying at the till, the assistant realizes to his horror that the washing machine is out of stock. You are frustrated and not a little angry that the sales assistant has wasted your time. Making amends, the assistant points out that the next model up *is* in stock and that he will sell it to you for the same price as the other model. At a stroke, he has redeemed himself. Such a service combines the best of people empowerment and management.

In practical terms this means that priorities are evaluated in the light of the potential business impact of service failure as opposed to merely meeting an internal – usually arbitrary – technical target. So the first question when engaging with a new customer is 'What is important to you?' The next question should be: 'What is important to your customers?'

Consider another example: an old-style service may have an agreement that software support calls are answered within one minute at the service desk and passed to engineers within five minutes, who must respond in four hours. This is fine as far as it goes, but perhaps there could be a solution that would eliminate the support calls altogether – for instance, by introducing online tutorials or simpler software interfaces, or even eliminating the use of the software completely by designing an improved business process.

Nurture your supply chain

Inevitably, what your company can offer is limited by what your suppliers can offer you. You may empower your staff to create excellent services for your customers, but unless your suppliers can also back your service flexibly then your staff may not be as empowered as they think. A local food shop, for example, may be reliant on logistics companies to deliver the food and drinks it sells on to the public. In cases of bad weather, if the lorry cannot get through, the shop's supplies may become exhausted.

No company alone can support the entire needs of its customers exclusively from its own resources. We have learned that nurturing and maximizing the benefits of your own supply chain are vital in being able to supply your customers with living service. For the food shop, some contingency in its choice of supplier and method of supply – to allow for easy adaptation and evolution – may be in order. After all, the shop's customers will blame the shop itself, not its suppliers, if they cannot buy the food they require. Supply chain relationships are often fraught with difficulties, as both parties seeking short-term financial benefit take on adversarial roles. Over the long term, this strategy could erode the ability of your supply chain to support you in serving your customers. A better way may be not to squeeze your suppliers on price, which limits their long-term capability, but to let them keep a healthy margin as part of an agreement to improve their services continually.

The difficulties that can occur when taking a short-term approach to suppliers can be seen in the UK supermarket sector. Having squeezed milk producers' margins ever more tightly over the past ten years, UK supermarkets realized that they were actually driving farms to switch their production out of dairy and into other areas. In order to ensure that their customers were looked after, supermarkets began to take a longer-term view of their dairy suppliers and unilaterally increased their offer prices to farmers. The result was happier suppliers and secure supplies. The president of the National Farmers' Union, Peter Kendall, described one such move as 'the most significant and encouraging development in the dairy industry for a very long time'.[3]

All service organizations should look at who they rely on to support their customers, and ensure that these organizations form a coalition to support their customers. These relationships should also include feedback into the supply chain of customers' needs and issues, thus increasing the scope with which new solutions can be developed.

Fujitsu's collaborations with its suppliers have often led to solutions that simply would not have happened if we had operated relationships purely at one level. We work closely with a number of global technology suppliers, such as Microsoft, SAP, Oracle, Cisco, Nokia and Sun. An example of a service developed in this way is unified communications. Unified communications enable people using different technologies to communicate with anyone, anywhere at any time. With a single identity, staff can seamlessly select and move between different modes of communication, choosing the most appropriate to the task in hand. For example, voicemail can be collected from an Outlook inbox, and video conferences can be initiated with a couple of clicks from within Outlook. The result is that staff can easily locate one another, communicate and collaborate regardless of geographic location. Organizations can also collaborate and communicate securely with suppliers and customers.

The service was developed with a number of suppliers and alliances, and is already providing value to customers. This arose out of the fact that, as organizations have come under greater pressure to be more competitive, cost-efficient and flexible, they have also become more fragmented and geographically dispersed. This poses a great communications challenge – even for companies leading the technological revolution. People now need to communicate across multiple locations, countries and time zones and have to contend with a disparate array of technologies from fixed and mobile voice telephones to email, instant messaging and video conferencing.

The creation of this service was only made possible by the combination of Fujitsu's and its suppliers' knowledge and expertise in software and managed services. Companies looking to transform themselves need to be open to collaboration for innovation. After all, nobody has a monopoly on great ideas.

Take the long-term view

Fujitsu is on an ongoing transformation journey. What we have learned so far is that initially we needed to set a direction and develop a service culture and a strategy (the Mind), then combine technological and process capabilities across the organization (the Body) and simultaneously maximize the energy of the whole organization (the Soul) to make it happen.

The results of this transformation, together with the emphasis on continual innovation, have resulted in an emphasis on creating a service culture which considers a long-term view as the only way of doing business. Indeed, we have found that it is only by developing long-term relationships that the customer has the time and space to co-create and evolve with the service provider the services they want.

Taking a short-term view of the relationship between a customer and supplier typically becomes a zero sum game – whatever the supplier gives away in financial discounts and extra services, the customer gains and vice versa, building a conflict of interest into the relationship. In the short term the size of the cake is limited to what it is today, and both parties logically attempt to maximize their share. This short-term self-interest works against cooperation. Taking a long-term view provides the opportunity for both the service provider and the customer to engage in strategies to increase the size of the cake for the benefit of both parties, allowing both to prosper.

A lot has been said and written about the merits of having a long-term perspective. Yet many companies, and just as importantly executives, remain too focused on the short term. Short-termism can work against developing a service culture and destroy trust. By striving extra hard to meet customer expectations today, you may suffer a short-term loss, but with an eye on long-term gain for both of you. It is easy to say that you are a business partner, but when it comes to the crunch you must be willing and able to act as one.

Difficulties can come when there are other stakeholders in the company who would prefer short-term gain. There could be some shareholders, for example, who want to maximize short-term profits and as a result could prevent a company from taking a longer term view of its customers. This means service providers wanting to provide living service should proactively engage in communication with shareholders and garner their support for longer-term growth.

A final argument for needing to embed long-term thinking is that to deliver great service today you need to have planned yesterday – or preferably the day before. So providers must not just look at what serves their customers today, but should work to understand what they may want tomorrow, and organize themselves and their supply chain to make this happen. A living service culture fosters innovation throughout all of an organization's activities. Innovation is not a discrete activity, but an integral and vital part of the whole service journey.

How do you anticipate what customers might be asking for in the future? Simple: by listening and talking to them. In Fujitsu, by sharing roadmaps, ongoing developments and innovations, we work with customers in developing future scenarios. This is enabling us to transform ourselves today and so serve our customers better in the future.

An example of this is a service Fujitsu provides to a bank in Japan. In order to deliver additional security when a customer wants to use an ATM, Fujitsu has developed a Palm Vein Authentication System. This futuristic device hygienically and efficiently reads palms and enables quick and accurate authentication prior to making a transaction. While not all companies can have a substantial R&D budget, a scalable long-term attitude towards continuous innovation is a key attribute of living service for any company.

There is an old management adage that says if you want to improve something, measure it. Management guru, Peter Drucker once said, 'If you can't measure it, you can't manage it'. Whatever an organization formally measures becomes a long-term focus point for the people working there. By simply measuring costs they find that costs reduce as awareness develops among staff. In a typical organization, how often is progress against sales targets measured? Every day? Every week? Every quarter? Rarely is it less frequent than this, and hence sales performance becomes a clear focus for most companies. However, customer satisfaction, which is at least partly responsible for delivering these results, is rarely measured every six months! By building a systematic way continually to measure customer service and advertise its results, an organization will automatically begin to focus the attention of people towards this important area.

Any organization measuring customer satisfaction should be striving to achieve top marks. Getting a satisfaction score of 8 out of 10 may sound fine and probably won't lose you the business in the short term, but what it shows is that there is a mismatch developing between you and the customer, a mismatch that the customer may not yet be able to articulate, other than by saying that they are feeling a little dissatisfied. It is only through people paying attention to them at this time, helping them to clarify their thoughts and then pushing the rest of the organization to act on the results, that the gap can be closed again. In this way, the service continues to reinvent itself to deliver business value, process efficiency and waste elimination on an ongoing basis.

A service provider should not engage in innovation only when prompted to by customer feedback. Armed with their specialist knowledge and roadmaps they can also proactively look at their customers' long-term strategies. You need to offer options which help move your customers towards their objectives. These might involve service improvements that the customer simply may not (or could not) have known about and could not have accessed otherwise.

In summary

We have learned that service providers need to put their customers at the centre of everything. Service providers need to appreciate how processes and technology work together to make great service. Combining these elements with a long-term view maximizes benefits for customers and their customers by producing services that can flex to their continually evolving needs.

Overall, the message from our journey so far is simple: living service is always about fitting the service to the customer; not trying to fit the customer to the service.

Agenda 1 – Develop a Living Service Culture

◆ Everything you do, do around customers and their customers
◆ Earn the trust of your customers and employees
◆ Put people at the centre of everything
◆ Empower champions of change
◆ Nurture your supply chain
◆ Take the long-term view

CHAPTER 2

Changing the Game

I n the previous chapter, we looked at ways of developing a living service culture. That is the starting point for the journey to living service. In this chapter, we shall now explain how we are doing things differently – or changing the game.

Think back to how Toyota transformed the automotive industry with its approach to lean production. The idea that you build quality into every component – rather than checking for quality after the car is built – seems obvious now. But, at the time, the thinking behind management ideas such as Total Quality Management was revolutionary. The Toyota Production System (TPS) changed the game for car manufacturers. But it also changed the expectations of everyone who drives a car. Today, we expect reliability as a given.

In fact, TPS changed manufacturing forever. We believe that by co-creating a journey with the customer, reducing complexity, delivering invisible excellence and elegant simplicity, living service has the potential to transform services forever too. As well as elaborating on these points, this chapter will discuss how living service can change the game comprehensively.

The modern world is full of service providers. No matter what your need, there is probably someone out there with a service that meets it. It could be an IT or logistics solution for a large company, or it could be wedding planning advice for a young couple, tax advice for a small business, or simply providing electricity to a family home. Whatever the service a bewildering array of service providers are only too pleased to help. So much choice makes the customer's task difficult – whether they want to get a broadband connection for their family PC or to outsource the IT needs of an entire multinational company. The problem is that until you start using a service it is difficult to know how well it matches your needs.

Traditional forms of service are not always noted for innovative thinking. Extended warranty companies, for example, offer to replace or repair a product if there is a problem. But the list of what is and what is not covered within the warranty is tightly prescriptive. The warranty will not change or evolve depending on market trends. The customer has no option to renegotiate after signing.

Within the corporate sphere an IT service company may offer what is known as a service 'wrap' around a product (such as a set of servers or desktop computers) which it provides to a customer. The term 'wrap' should immediately set alarm bells ringing. It suggests that the product itself is the focus and the service is almost incidental. Such a wrap may offer various service-level agreements should the product break down, but it may not provide any roadmap to the future in terms of providing upgrades or enhancements. Indeed, in many cases the wrap is an additional revenue stream for the supplier rather than a genuine attempt to co-create an evolving service with the customer. In other words, it is a service which is product-feature-driven and does not adapt to the changing circumstances. This is a dying service – and there are a lot of them about. Ask yourself: as a supplier how can you do things differently, for your customers and their customers?

Another way to understand inflexible, dying service is to consider how banks and other financial organizations have changed in the last few years. It used to be that high street banks around the world opened between 9 am and 5 pm, Monday to Friday. Want to check your bank account in the evening? Forget it. Want an appointment to consider a new mortgage on a Saturday afternoon as you work full time during the week? Think again. In this circumstance, the product – banking – was centred very firmly around the bank itself rather than the customer.

And yet, in banking times have changed. From the 1970s onwards, ATMs made it possible to withdraw money and access other simple banking services around the clock. In the 1980s, in some countries, branches started opening on Saturdays and sometimes even Sundays, with appointments being particularly easy to book on those days. Recently, the internet has made it possible to view all your accounts and access any service from the comfort of your own home at any time of the day or night. A combination of people working in branches, as well as internet and ATM technology – art and science – has moved the service very firmly back towards the customer. As a result, banking service today is far more responsive and adaptable to the needs and requirements of customers. The green shoots of a living service are beginning to grow as the banks have learned to do things differently.

Within this context, all companies face a challenge to differentiate themselves from the competition. Sometimes this differentiation might be a small improvement in the service offered. Think, for example, of a super-market that starts to employ people to pack customers' bags. Typically, such a service – if successful – is adopted by its rivals. So, in time, competing supermarkets in the area will also offer a bag-packing service. The differentiator is eroded.

But sometimes a company makes a big change to its service offering which alters the game. This allows it to stake out a fundamentally new market space. According to the leading marketing thinker, Philip Kotler:

> Good companies will meet needs; great companies will create markets. Market leadership is gained by envisioning new products, services, lifestyles, and ways to raise living standards. There is a vast difference between companies that offer me-too products and those that create new product and service values not even imagined by the marketplace. Ultimately, marketing at its best is about value creation and raising the world's living standards. [1]

There are examples of this in every industry. In their book *Blue Ocean Strategy*, W. Chan Kim and Renée Mauborgne define this quantum leap into new market space as being akin to jumping from a crowded red ocean to a clear, competition-free blue ocean. One example they identify is Accor, the French hotel group. Accor changed the face of budget hotels across Europe by creating the Formule 1 chain – a mass-market standardized bed and breakfast operation which offered 2-star quality but at 1-star prices. Managers at Accor were able to do this by rethinking what people actually need from budget hotels. They got rid of surplus restaurants, lounges, desks and stationery in rooms, and introduced rooms built in modular blocks (high quality with low cost) and much improved beds. In short, the customer got a much better night's sleep at a much cheaper price.[2] Service quality was improved and costs reduced. The result was a quantum leap in economy accommodation. In other words, Formule 1 changed the game in the budget hotel market across Europe forever.

So how do you change the game? How do you see things from your customer's perspective? We believe that the starting point and the first key difference of living service from conventional service models is the importance of making customers' needs transparent. What we mean by this is getting close to really understanding what it is the customer is after.

Make customers' needs transparent

Traditionally, suppliers may have provided only a feature-oriented list from which the customer chooses the service which matches their needs as closely as possible. By contrast, a living service takes as its starting point exactly what the customer needs and then flexes the service around that.

In the previous chapter we saw that while service delivery methodologies, price-lists and other elements of the deal were important, the service that ASIC (Allianz Shared Infrastructure Services) valued the most when they decided to outsource their workplace, net and telecommunication services was looking after the people who were to be outsourced, as the supplier would soon be responsible for looking after them.

Other customers may have different priorities. A typical customer may want his car to be the same colour as his garage door for instance. A wealthy customer may want her car to be the same colour as her yacht. In all cases, the service provider needs to be able to ask the right questions and align with the customer to bring these needs out. It is only by doing this that great service can be delivered. Furthermore, if this alignment does not occur from the start, the service provider and the customer cannot grow together.

Grow together with customers and their customers

Any service provider wants to create and grow long-lasting relationships with customers as these help provide strategic direction both to itself and its customers. After all, this will enhance business opportunities and foster long-term sustainable service innovation.

At each of the stages – which we later label as sell, solve, deliver and innovate – you must constantly look to understand, honour and respond properly to the Mind-Body-Soul of the customer.

The use of the word honour within the concept of the Mind-Body-Soul dynamic may sound out of place in a business context. Respect for people is probably a more familiar phrase. But in Japan, honour is a very important idea. It may sound anachronistic, but it implies a sense of reverence and duty beyond mere respect that informs every interaction with the customer. We believe this is also a crucial element within business today. It recognizes that the service provider and customer are embarking on a journey together. This forms the basis for a long-term relationship, which will ultimately benefit not just the supplier and customer but also the customer's customer.

Let's now look at an example of growing together with a customer. DMR, formerly a major Canada-based consulting group and now a Fujitsu company, started working with a major US manufacturer in the aerospace industry in 1989.

The company's IT division wanted a system delivery lifecycle service to facilitate its project management and delivery processes.

Following a successful tender, Fujitsu delivered a methodology called Productivity Plus. Over the years, the methodology has undergone many adaptations and evolutions. Today, it is known as Macroscope and is contributing across the manufacturer's IT department as a core methodology.

The relationship has grown. From 1994 onwards, recognizing Fujitsu's project management and system architecture skills, the manufacturer started to employ some of these expert resources for its own projects. Then the relationship developed further as Fujitsu was asked to take over the maintenance of various applications. And then, from 1998, Fujitsu started to provide custom built packages for the customer.

With a continually growing relationship for more than 18 years, an enormous level of tacit knowledge is now shared between the manufacturer and Fujitsu. This knowledge has grown through interactions between people at all levels of the organization, as well as the pooling of information, as people work side-by-side on a wide range of projects.

A virtuous circle has emerged between Fujitsu, the customer and the customer's customers. All benefit from the relationship.

The best relationships are those that endure and provide mutual bene-fit. Key to this is the ability to update and refine existing internal processes as experience grows. In other words, there is a two-way symbi-otic flow of knowledge between the sell, solve, deliver and innovate areas to the mutual benefit of the service provider, the customer and the cus-tomer's customers.

A famous version of symbiosis is the relationship of the Egyptian plover bird and the crocodile. In this relationship, the bird is well known for prey-ing on parasites that feed on crocodiles and are potentially harmful to them. To that end, the crocodile openly invites the bird to hunt on its body, even going so far as to open its jaws to allow the bird to enter the mouth safely to hunt. For the bird's part, this relationship is not only a ready source of food, but is a safe one considering that few predator species would dare strike at the bird at such proximity to its fearsome host.

Whether you are a plover or a crocodile, a long-lasting, evolving rela-tionship can provide long-term benefits to all parties.

In many respects, living service challenges the conventional service model. But in place of a quantum leap, it brings incremental improve-ments. The service is continually evolving. In place of a static, feature-led dying service, there is a people-centred living service, which adapts and evolves to customers' needs. This is the fundamental difference with living service – it never sleeps but is on a path of continuous innovation.

People-centred relationships are vital for longer-term partnerships with customers and a capability to provide a living service for customers and their customers. We have learned that this difference echoes the ideas of Professors Kim and Mauborgne to seek value innovation by leaving a crowded red ocean and discovering a new blue ocean market space. By acting differently in this way, competition is made irrelevant. So how can such differentiated services be identified? How can you design services that will excite your customers?

The answer to this is simply to look at things from the customer's point of view. It sounds obvious and a lot of companies would say they already do this. But in our experience very few organizations have truly adopted this way of thinking. The step from designing services around products to designing services around customers is a huge one.

Companies must think harder about how customers would like to see their service designed, contracted and delivered. It is only by making this leap that the true benefits and power of living service can be harnessed. Services that are truly built with the customer at the centre automatically move in tandem with the customer – they flex and adapt to the customer's ever-changing environment. The entire journey can then be co-created as a platform for growth. Providers of living service are also able to anticipate changes in the customer's world – and help them respond before these happen.

Consider people as your key differentiator

Beyond the need to grow together with our customers, changing the game requires us continually to consider people as the key differentiator. In the previous chapter we discussed how the seeds of the relationship with Reuters were created. Let us now continue that story to illustrate the next key element of game changing – that of putting people at the centre of everything. After all, a strategic mindset is one thing, having the people in place to deal with the result is quite another.

In the words of Bill Simpson, the Fujitsu account director, a 'change agent' within Reuters was needed to help drive the agenda forward. Such an agent was personified in David Lister, who joined as CIO in November 2004. The first meeting between Simpson and Lister was pivotal. In a no-nonsense, straight-talking manner they both described the difficulties with the existing contracts and service from their respective positions. By doing this they were able to build up trust and begin to understand each other's issues.

To win the confidence of the new CIO Fujitsu needed opportunities to deliver on its promise of driving up service quality. The first test of this relationship came with the initiative to move 3,000 Reuters employees from many London offices to its new global headquarters in Canary Wharf. Fujitsu was asked to manage much of the technology provision, the desktop move and the implementation of new IT services in the new headquarters. As Reuters operates in such a fast-moving, dynamic environment – after all news never sleeps – there was no margin for error in the delivery.

Fujitsu delivered this project on time and in budget. It was essential that the team adapted to the culture within Reuters, operating with the same levels of dynamism and fleetness of foot needed to meet the challenging timescales. For example, the project team had to adopt shift patterns to work around the editorial team within Reuters, so that business could run as usual. The key point is that the delivery aspect of the service only succeeded because the people delivering it were culturally sensitive, flexible and adaptable in their dealings with the customer. Respect for and response to the customer's cultural and people needs allowed the project to be executed successfully. In all, the project was completed in just 12 weeks and, apart from the delivery, included new phones, computers and printers, a news 'ticker' and a 40-foot (not inch) plasma television screen outside the building.

As a result, Fujitsu not only became a trusted service provider, but also showed it could align its people successfully with Reuters staff. By acting differently in a people-centred context and taking account of the cultural aspects of their customers, companies can leverage enormous service advantage. This can change the game completely and leave feature-oriented dying service for dust.

Leverage tacit knowledge

Another key difference in the way living service operates from the conventional service model is the value it places on tacit knowledge. At a high level, tacit knowledge is the collection of all the things that we know *how* to do but perhaps cannot easily explain. In a seminal *Harvard Business Review* article, Professor Ikujiro Nonaka, a globally renowned scholar in knowledge creating theories, wrote:

> *Tacit knowledge is highly personal. It is hard to formalize and, therefore, difficult to communicate to others ... Tacit knowledge is also deeply rooted in action and in an individual's commitment to a specific context – a craft or profession, a particular technology or product market or the activities of a group or team ... A master craftsman after years of experience develops a wealth of expertise 'at his fingertips.' But he is often unable to articulate the scientific or technical principles behind what he knows.*[3]

What Nonaka suggests is that it is important to realize that the management of explicit knowledge alone will not suffice in today's business environment. We have found that often the difference between high performance and average performance rests in elements which are not explicit but tacit in their understandings.

Nonaka has written about the case of Nippon Roche, part of the Roche group, a multinational healthcare group based in Switzerland. The company was going through a difficult time thanks to low market growth, fierce competition and institutional changes in the healthcare industry.[4] In response, the company launched a programme to learn more about customer needs and create better solutions. It did so by seeking to improve the skills of its key sales people – the medical representatives (MRs). While traditional training had focused on conventional best practice, such as role-playing to improve performance, it had been realized that these techniques were inadequate to facilitate the sharing of tacit knowledge between individuals. To encourage sales innovation, the new project sought to distil the skills of the high performing MRs and to transfer them to the ones performing at a lower level.

According to Nonaka, Nippon Roche recognized that high performers tend to have better tacit skills. For example, they are more effective about knowing the good and not so good times to meet particular doctors (effectively the customers to the MRs). In addition, high performing MRs use a variety of sources when carrying out the research necessary for their job and have clear targets in their minds. In order to get this knowledge shared with the average performers, the high performers produced a new sales manual. This synthesized tacit and explicit knowledge by using metaphors and stories. Such stories are useful as they help people to understand their own thinking and capture the context. To supplement this, a variety of on-the-job training, workshops, experience exchange meetings and coaching was given to the average performers.

The result was that sales performance soared after the project was completed in January 2000. Nippon Roche concluded that the participants of the project had become 'more valuable assets to the company'. From a situation where many average performers were neglecting customer needs, just making product calls and not taking notes, a new breed of high performing, customer-focused MRs emerged. They had acquired the tacit knowledge to interact with customers by seeking timely appointments focusing on the doctors' needs.

As Nonaka concluded, by appreciating the human value of tacit knowledge, Nippon Roche created an environment where salespeople became far more in tune with their customers in terms of process and output. By changing the game away from just focusing on the explicit, Nippon Roche created a key differentiator.

Focus on invisible excellence and elegant simplicity

By appreciating the importance of proper alignment, understanding customer needs and maximizing tacit knowledge, a company can deliver both invisible excellence and elegant simplicity for the customer. These are key competitive differentiators in any market. When complexity is reduced the service can become seamless and so offer the end-customer (the customer's customer) a coherent living service.

One of the companies we know well is Whitbread. Founded in 1742, the core of its business is now four brands: Premier Inns, the UK's largest budget hotel chain with 500 hotels and over 33,000 hotel rooms; the Costa Coffee chain of over 700 coffee shops; and the Beefeater and Brewer's Fayre pub/restaurants which together have almost 400 restaurants.

Whitbread's vision is to become 'the best hospitality company there is'. This is delivered by a team of 35,000 employees involved in delivering services to 8.5 million customers a month. At the heart of how Whitbread delivers service is the 'Whitbread Way'. This is described by Whitbread as being 'like DNA'.

It's a common thread running throughout the company but it definitely doesn't mean we are all the same. Just like a family is made up of different people, each with their own individual look and character, so are our brands all different and each one has its own unique personality or brand values. We believe in people and teamwork; caring for guests; passion for winning; and continuous innovation.

This is music to our ears. But Whitbread is a highly complex business. Consider something as straightforward as a kitchen order printer for instance. A kitchen printer is a relatively inexpensive piece of equipment.

But if one stops functioning at a Beefeater on a Sunday lunchtime it can create mayhem in the kitchen. So this one piece of equipment could ruin the service to dozens of Whitbread's customers who may the following week be tempted to try somewhere else.

The business impact of outages and failures can be even more severe if they hit at the wrong time of the week or year. Beefeater and Brewer's Fayre are busier through the weekends, whereas Premier Inns are busier during the week when network and system availability is critical during busy check-in periods. The time of year is also important in the hospitality industry. The restaurants, as is common across the industry, can make as much as half of their annual revenues in the weeks leading up to and including the Christmas holidays.

So what can be done about this? The answer is that Fujitsu – which provides many IT services to Whitbread – needed not only to understand the implication of what they were contractually responsible for, but also to align more effectively their service to the overall strategy, enabling technology, processes and people – or Mind, Body and Soul – of Whitbread. To achieve this, a member of Fujitsu's delivery team, be it an account manager, service delivery manager or a project officer, was on site at Whitbread's HQ every single day. On the face of it this may not be a productive use of their specialist skills, but the value of this continual interaction was that Whitbread was assured that its services were supplied by someone who was committed to being in-tune with its needs and understood the impact on its business.

Words may express only 10 per cent of the image a customer has in mind. To understand the other 90 per cent such continual interaction is necessary to capture the tacit dimension of a customer's needs. Knowledge cannot be gleaned from simply studying documentation, such as organizational charts and work plans. Continual interaction with Whitbread was key. As a result of all these activities the service has been significantly improved so that now not only is Whitbread getting what it originally contracted for, it is actually getting a level of service that allows it to deliver an even better service to its own customers. By developing its relationship with Whitbread, Fujitsu has evolved itself to meet Whitbread's business needs. More thought and resources have been focused on effective peak planning to ensure that at busy times of the week and year

Fujitsu can respond to Whitbread's needs. Again, this has been driven by Whitbread allowing Fujitsu to see how important this is for its business.

The lessons of this story are clear: by acting in a different manner – by really seeking to understand, honour and respond to the complete needs of its customers – a great service can be provided to a customer and its customers.

In summary

While we have talked of many specific ways the game can be changed – making customers' needs transparent, growing together with customers and their customers, considering people as the key differentiator, leveraging tacit knowledge and focusing on elegant simplicity and invisible excellence – the key is that service must always adapt and evolve to deliver the needs of the customer and their customer. Without appreciating this central point, the game cannot even be started, let alone changed. In the next part of the book (Body), we will elaborate on how living service delivers to the evolving needs of the customer. This will be done by considering the processes and enabling technologies in the four key areas of business – sell, solve, deliver and innovate – which we will describe using our Four Row Model.

Agenda 2 – Change the Game

◆ Make customers' needs transparent

◆ Grow together with customers and their customers

◆ Consider people as your key differentiator

◆ Leverage tacit knowledge

◆ Focus on invisible excellence and elegant simplicity

PART 2

Body 体 Karada

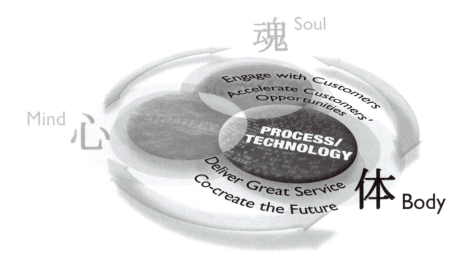

In human beings, the body is the physical part that enables us to act on the mind's decisions using energy from the soul. The same is true in our concept of living service.

This part consists of the physical structure of people, processes and technologies that allows a customer's needs to flow to provide a service outcome. How easily and accurately this flow occurs and how appropriately the Body responds to it is inextricably linked with both the Mind and the Soul.

The organization of the Body must be aligned to allow the flow of customer's needs to run through it and for the needs to be honoured and responded to at every stage.

This part is divided into four chapters:

Chapter 3: Engaging with Customers – this chapter focuses on understanding the customers' journey and managing the ongoing relationship.

Chapter 4: Accelerating Customers' Opportunities – having listened to the customer, a service must be developed to meet the customers' needs.

Chapter 5: Delivering Great Service – following on from development, this chapter is about ensuring delivery is continually in tune with customers and their customers' needs.

Chapter 6: Co-creating the Future – this chapter looks at enabling continuous innovation throughout the journey with customers.

Within Fujitsu, a model has been developed to ensure that the customer is at the centre of everything we do. We call it the Four Row Model. The rows are **sell, solve, deliver** and **innovate**. We believe that any service business needs to contain four fundamental stages in order to thrive throughout the journey with the customer. First, a service provider needs to engage with the customer in order to **sell** services. Secondly, they need to **solve** their customer's problems in order to accelerate the customer's opportunities. Thirdly, the provider simply needs to **deliver** great service. Finally, the service provider needs to continually **innovate** in order to co-create the future with the customer.

Let us now explain this model through the use of an analogy.

A bakery's journey

Imagine a baker in a small town. He had for many years supplied simple white loaves to his customers. His customers loved them and their demands meant that over time he improved the set-up of his bakery to provide more loaves more efficiently. Sometimes he had a problem. A regular customer would make a request for something special like a birthday cake. The baker's problem was that to do this he would have to disrupt his normal schedule, as his bakery was not really set up to bake cakes. He would still bake them, but these cakes would take him a long time, were expensive and sometimes didn't turn out exactly right. He simply didn't have the same combination of experience, ingredients and tools for cakes as he did have for making white loaves. Despite these problems, the baker's focus on customer service built him a good reputation and he was well known in the local community. Eventually, after many years the baker decided to retire.

The baker had four children who decided that together they could run and grow their father's business successfully in the future, while retaining the excellent reputation built by their father. The four of them had very distinct preferences and skills, but felt that together this was something they could do.

The eldest son was Stuart. Since childhood he had never really enjoyed baking as he found it lonely kneading dough at 4 am, but his gregarious and enthusiastic attitude was perfectly suited to being in the shop, talking to customers and keeping them happy. Stuart specialized in selling.

Second oldest was Sally. Sally loved baking and cooking. She'd always helped her father in the early mornings. After school she also won a place at catering college where she gained an in-depth expertise in many aspects of baking. Often when her father had been trying to come up with something special for a customer, Sally was the one who put together a solution. Sally's speciality was solving.

Sally's younger brother was Des. He didn't have Sally's creative streak, but Des enjoyed seeing how the ovens produced such big trays of bread. As a child he always thought that he wanted to put even more bread on each tray. As he grew up, this drove him to attend college too, but unlike Sally he studied production engineering. Using his knowledge he had been able to streamline his father's baking processes to increase white bread-making capacity by 20 per cent. Des's role was delivering.

The youngest in the family was Imogen. Imogen had something of an entrepreneurial streak. As a child she had taken her father's bread rolls to school and, along with Stuart, sold them to classmates (hence opening up new markets). She had also got her father to bake these rolls in the shape of cartoon characters (hence innovating products) as she thought these would sell better. And she was right: her fellow pupils bought as many as Stuart was able to carry to school, so Imogen even got Stuart to take a cart to school! Imogen was focused on innovating.

On the day of their father's retirement the four children decided to sit down and work out how they would be able to expand the business to support all of them and their own families into the future. They realized that the only way to do this was to sell more products and so they turned to Stuart (selling) and asked him what he needed in order to do this. Stuart said he'd find out what customers wanted and what they would pay for. He said that they should then organize themselves in response to their customer's needs.

Stuart went out and began to talk with customers. He quickly discovered that there seemed to be lots of opportunities to sell them more products. He found that customers wanted to buy more white loaves if the bakery could only supply them. Also, as there were lots of birthday parties, picnics and weddings, customers wanted other baked goods too. Stuart didn't know which products would fit their needs best for these events, or what sort of quantities they should produce, but he wrote down his findings and went to see Sally (solving) to see if she could solve these problems for him.

Sally looked at Stuart's findings. She realized that before she could decide what products they should look at making she'd need to ask some more detailed questions of the customers directly. So she spent some time in the shop and found out in greater detail about customers' needs. What did they want to do at a party or picnic? What were the outcomes that they wanted at these events? What was important to them and the other people at these events (their customers' customers)? She listened carefully and afterwards felt that there were a lot of new recipes she'd have to work on, from brown bread and cakes to sausage rolls and doughnuts. She had seen that there was a massive demand from customers but what she wasn't sure of was how it could all be baked while still guaranteeing the quality standards that had built their father's reputation. As it was, the ovens in the bakery were already at full stretch delivering the current demand. Luckily, Sally knew just the person to see – Des (delivering).

Des looked at Sally's recipes. He knew that the various customer demands were too much for the existing ovens. So he wondered if Sally might put more detail into her recipes so that he could test them. If they worked, he could then send some of the simpler recipes like brown bread off to a larger bakery to make and then deliver the bread back. If the recipes were detailed enough the large bakery would produce them at the same quality they would have produced themselves. He also set up a process whereby they could test what the large bakery produced.

Des found that some of the items were a little too specialized for them at the moment. For example, as they had no experience with meat, sausage rolls were better handled by someone else. This would let Des concentrate on making the celebration cakes and other more bespoke items using their own ovens. These cakes had no written detailed recipes but relied on Sally's expertise – tacit knowledge – as each was unique. Just baking these cakes was a challenge, so he hired a few people to help in the back of the bakery.

Within a few weeks they were selling more products than ever before. Customers were overjoyed that their needs were being met so well and word spread about the bakery with its great service. Stuart was busy working on the counter and stocking the shop windows while keeping customers informed of the new products. Sally was capturing needs, designing new products, giving them to Stuart to test with customers. If customers liked the new products, Des was getting Sally to develop recipes so that he could send them out to suppliers or get his own staff to follow them.

Sally was continuing to talk to customers and capture their needs in ever greater detail. She had noticed that for her various celebration cakes, such as the birthday, wedding and anniversary cakes, customers often wanted the same sponge filling but with a different icing design depending on the celebration. Knowing that the sponge was an important part of these cakes, Sally spent considerable time and effort in developing a recipe for the very best sponge filling. She gave this to Des. Des sent the recipe out to one of his suppliers who could now deliver these sponge cake bases back to the bakery. One of Des's assistants would then decorate them with icing.

Sally had also noticed that, although the icing would be different for each of these celebration cakes, if she asked the same questions of customers they could guide the design themselves. So she would find out, for example, what sort of celebration it was and what the name, age and sex of the recipient was. She was making her customers' needs transparent. She captured these questions, the range of answers and the different designs that they would provide in a document. This allowed others with Sally's level of skills to design cake icing by simply following the steps she had designed, rather than having to work it out from scratch. Over time Sally further noticed how certain cake designs were requested again and again. The 21st birthday cake was particularly popular. As a result, she made a specific recipe for a 21st birthday cake, making the baking of this particular cake even faster.

This new process took output from just 6 celebration cakes a day to 18 and, as the assistants were now focused purely on icing cakes, their tacit knowledge and skills grew very quickly. The new scale of production also meant that Des could invest in specialist icing equipment to make their work even quicker, easier and of higher quality. Not only were more customers being served, they were being better served!

By now Des was responsible for producing hundreds of products a day but, as he was able to provide his suppliers with detailed recipes, quality was strictly controlled. Soon though, Stuart and Sally started to discover customer needs that no one had ever met before, such as savoury birthday cakes, and sweet and sour doughnuts. Des then had to deliver these. Fortunately as Des had made his delivery of products so elegantly simple, he was able to give these unusual requests more time and attention, which meant he could successfully deliver them with the same level of invisible excellence as all the other bread and cakes. So popular in fact were the savoury birthday cakes that demand grew, but Des couldn't find a supplier who could make them. So he set up his own production facility using Sally's recipe for savoury birthday cakes as a basis. This turned out to be the first of many production facilities that Des set up to make Sally's new recipes.

The business was doing really well. The demands on Stuart, Sally and Des were tough. They were kept so busy with their key activities – selling, solving and delivering – that they had little time to look at how they might further improve their own individual work or the work of the business as a whole. So they turned to their youngest sister, Imogen (innovating), to help.

Imogen had watched her siblings develop the business from being a simple supplier of white loaves to being able to identify the most unusual customer needs and deliver against them successfully and economically. She could see how her family was struggling to grow further, so she set out to help. First she realized that the shop was limited in what it could sell. The queues were getting longer as customers came from further away. So she went out and set up new shops and provided them with sales staff (similar to Stuart) and, occasionally, local experts (similar to Sally), which had the effect of opening up new markets for the business.

Within a few weeks Imogen began to see that customer requests coming in from the new shops had similarities that could possibly be made into standard recipes by Sally for delivery by Des. She spoke to Stuart about these new product ideas and between them they talked about what they thought would sell and what would not, and consequently what should and should not be developed. In doing this Imogen was helping Stuart keep what he was selling up to date and relevant to customers.

Imogen also went out to find new ingredients for Sally's recipes to help meet customers' needs better. New organic flours and free-range eggs all helped Sally meet evolving customer's needs. Imogen also went out to find suppliers who could help Des improve in delivery. She investigated new ovens, better wrapping that kept the food fresh for longer, and faster mixing machines, all of which helped Des to deliver.

Imogen's new ideas helped all her siblings, making their lives considerably easier and allowing them to focus on their own key activities. She also opened up new markets with the new shops. In effect Imogen had become responsible for shaping the strategy for the company's future. Sometimes these strategic areas were identified by customers making their needs known or suppliers offering new products, but at other times Imogen decided on her own initiatives in order to grow the business. As a result the bakery grew, first locally and then nationally.

After a few years the bakery had grown in both size and capability, and served customers across the country and met their needs better. The baker's children were pleased that they had been able to do this while never compromising on the quality that their father's first bakery had built its reputation on. The relentless pursuit of the children to understand, honour and respond to their customers' changing needs provided them with many happy customers.

In summary

The bakery story provides an example of a service organized to make customer needs transparent, to focus on invisible excellence and elegant simplicity, and to continually adapt and evolve to meet customer needs. The baker's children were successful in achieving their goals. To do so they aligned their mind, body and soul together and with their customers.

The Four Row Model

As briefly mentioned at the beginning of this section, Fujitsu's Four Row Model has been developed to ensure that the customer is at the centre of everything (see Figure 3.1). The rows (or stages) are **sell** [Row 1], **solve** [Row 2], **deliver** [Row 3] **and innovate** [Row 4].

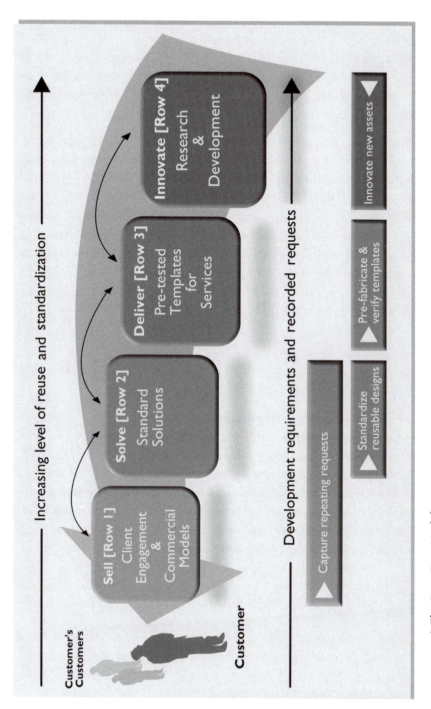

FIGURE 3.1 ◆ The Four Row Model

In this model the service provider is aligned to the customer at each stage (sell, solve, deliver, innovate) of the journey. Energy also flows between the rows themselves. These flows allow service providers to capture customers' evolving needs and process them through the rows into deliverable solutions. And simultaneously they allow the service provider continually to drive innovative services towards the customer.

- *Sell* [Row 1] Engaging with Customers – in our baker's story, this was Stuart's job. He was focused on building and continuing relationships with existing and new customers in order to understand their needs and promote appropriate services.

- *Solve* [Row 2] Accelerating Customers' Opportunities – this was Sally's job. Building on Stuart's knowledge and experience, she refined understanding of their customers' evolving needs. She then developed and continually updated solutions to meet these needs.

- *Deliver* [Row 3] Delivering Great Service – Des fulfilled this role. Once Sally developed her solutions, Des delivered them.

- *Innovate* [Row 4] Co-creating the Future – delivering today does not necessarily secure the future. Imogen had to innovate new services by taking input from all her siblings, as well as from suppliers and customers. This allowed her to develop new ideas for existing and new markets.

These four rows and the relationships between them deliver a living body for a living service. This results in the service provider, customer and their customer all having the time and space to co-create and evolve the service continually.

A key part of the Mind-Body-Soul triad is having the processes and technology (the Body) in place. These physical elements act on the mind's decisions using energy from the soul. It is these physical elements – the four rows – which will be the focus of our next four chapters.

CHAPTER 3

Engaging with Customers

Customer engagement is all about building and continuing the relationship between the service provider and the customer. This enables both the service provider and the customer to grow together by understanding the customer's journey. Also, by taking a consistent approach to the customer throughout the journey, a service provider can continually improve service to earn customer respect and loyalty.

This is in sharp contrast to the way in which many sales functions traditionally behave. A director of a major UK telecommunications company observed, 'Service providers tend to overreact with sales presentations adding a barrage of sales information ... we want a more evolutionary and strategic engagement.' Engagement with a long-term view is highly valued by customers.

Focus on understanding the customer's journey

A key attribute of providing living service is that you must understand your customer's journey. By continual engagement within the journey, the full scope of needs, now and in the future, are made transparent both to the customer themselves and to the service provider. A deep dive into the customer's soul is preferable to a shallow paddle.

Consider the following short story. It's Saturday morning and George is heading to the golf club for the first time. On arrival at the club house, he speaks to the club professional, James. James asks George how he could be of assistance. George explains that he'd like to use the driving range. James, not knowing that this is George's first time, points to the clubs and where the range is and simply explains the price. On noticing, however, that George picks up a putter instead of a driver, he gently enquiries if this is George's first time and whether he would like some further assistance.

George then explains how this is indeed his first time playing golf and he needs to learn quickly. This is in order not to frustrate his new, short-tempered boss by taking too long to finish the round that they have organized for next month.

In order to understand George's situation better, James asks some more questions. He finds out that George is generally a good sportsman and has no injuries. He also finds out that George is left-handed. He then measures George in order to provide the right clubs for his height. Finally, he asks a little more about how good George's boss is. On finding out that George's boss has a handicap of 25, he reassures George that his boss is not as good as he initially feared. As a result, he recommends that George comes in for two lessons a week and takes a putter home to practise every night before the match. This, James concludes, should be enough to allow George to stave off embarrassment (and ensure that his boss still wins!)

In this short story, James provided a service that was much better than George (who has gone in initially only to use the driving range) had ever thought possible. James did this by using his specialist skills and knowl-edge to understand and provide an appropriate response to George's situation. By understanding the journey that George was on, he was able to adapt the service for him to fit his needs better than George had thought was possible. To do this James had taken the time to find out about his past (his previous sporting experience and health), his present issue (how he should train for the match), and, finally, his future needs (the impending match and his boss's expertise).

When we have worked successfully with companies, we have engaged with them in much the same manner as James did with George. For example, understanding Allianz's recent history – as we saw in Chapter 1 – was key to working with the company. If Fujitsu had simply tried to understand Allianz's situation by taking a measure of its current business activities and the opportunities, we would not have understood the real situation the company was in.

Once you have understood the customer's journey, you can – and must – craft the solutions and support they need. Think back to the Reuters example. We have discussed the origins of the relationship and how, through the work of Bill Simpson and his account team, Fujitsu's and Reuters mindsets became more aligned. The result was that Fujitsu put together a bid to manage Reuters entire IT infrastructure late in 2006 and early 2007.

Our challenge was that although we delivered service to many customers globally Reuters needed service delivery in over 100 countries! To deliver great services to Reuters, Fujitsu needed to further extend its global delivery model. Without a compelling global model, the deal could not get off the ground. The vision simply could not be fulfilled.

What could be done to demonstrate adherence to the CIO's vision of global growth? The answer lay in utilizing Fujitsu's partners around the world. The purpose of this was to turn Fujitsu into a global 'aggregator' of service for Reuters instead of being a single supplier.

This approach had a distinct advantage. It meant that the company was offering something that was not reliant on a single service provider. Instead it was seeking to leverage the best partners from around the world. Most infrastructure components could be delivered with global suppliers, but local high-touch services needed best-in-region suppliers to be aligned under a Fujitsu service desk-led model. The value that Fujitsu would provide to Reuters would be as an aggregator of all these component elements which made up the full service. Such an approach is flexible and can ensure that the best suppliers are used in all the various regions of the world. Fujitsu's commitment to Reuters is to strive continually to drive service and price competitiveness from the aggregated suppliers over the life of the contract. A potential problem was turned into a dream team.

In order to sustain this proposal, three key elements were necessary. First, it was important for Fujitsu to make the service desk the absolute 'engine room of service'. This was because it is the service desk which is the first point of contact into the service for Reuters employees. If this goes wrong, then the overall service's reputation and reliability would take a huge knock. Secondly, Fujitsu worked hard to ensure that we and our partners understood Reuters journey. Existing relationships with Microsoft, Dell, Cisco and CA were leveraged and other vendors respected by Reuters were brought in, including Satyam, BT and SBS. Letters to the Reuters board from Steve Ballmer (CEO of Microsoft) and Michael Dell (founder and CEO at Dell) helped bolster the bid. Indeed, at the end – when the complex, global, transformational outsource was won – the Microsoft account manager wrote: 'I feel like the supplier of an ingredient, Fujitsu has just shown how the whole cake is baked.'

The final element was the need to demonstrate to Reuters the value of the approach. A showcase was held in London to demonstrate the overall capability that we could deliver. This was set up in just nine days. Partners including Microsoft, SBS, Dell and CA were there to demonstrate their ingredients. The event was akin to an innovation lab – a vision of the transformed state, and an opportunity to show how collaborations with customers and partners could work on an ongoing basis.

It worked. In August 2007, Fujitsu was awarded the £500 million, 10-year global outsourcing deal with Reuters. The deal was truly rewarding for all those involved at Fujitsu as it meant taking on, transforming and running Reuters internal IT infrastructure and corporate applications, supporting 17,500 Reuters employees in more than 100 countries and seeing some 500 staff transferred across 41 countries. An understanding of the customer's journey and an ability to flex our service around this had paid a huge dividend.

In order fully to understand the customers' journey, we have found the following pointers useful for people who are engaging with customers.

Be ready for some straight talking

Customers are not always fully aware of their own possibilities. They might think they know what they want, but as they often do not understand the full extent of what is possible, they might frame their needs within limits that do not actually exist. Often customers will draft their needs in terms of their existing experience. This usually does not take into account new innovations. In effect, they ask for a dying service.

As a result, it is common for the service provider, as a specialist in their field, to be able to add greater value than the customer themselves. The service provider must always look to deliver this extra value. This sometimes means challenging customers' existing assumptions with some straight talking.

Fujitsu has worked with a major European energy company for many years. We provide break-fix services (put simply, if something breaks we fix it) for computer hardware in the company's Exploration and Production division. Although the work together was long-standing, Fujitsu wanted to move from being a supplier to being a partner with enough access to the business to offer innovation for business improvement and increasing value. The difficulty was that the energy company's perception of Fujitsu had been built via the existing contract of low-level services. It did not see Fujitsu as a company that could add such value. This was a perception Fujitsu had to overcome.

In order to meet this challenge, a team inside Fujitsu started by asking what it was that the energy company actually did. What challenges did it face? Fujitsu realized that it had a much bigger set of services and products that might actually be of interest to its customer, as opposed to simply trying to extend the break-fix contract. After identifying a number of different areas in which Fujitsu might be able to assist, a joint seminar was held with 26 senior managers from the customer invited to Fujitsu's Research and Development Laboratories in Japan to look at the latest advances in supercomputing technology. This was something of which the company needed to stay abreast. Exploration and Production made up 60 per cent of profits for the group. As oil reserves nearer the earth's surface become used up, oil companies have to look ever deeper for their new supplies. They need the latest technologies to analyze with ever greater accuracy the seismic readings which help them decide where to drill. This means costs go up and new technologies that can find oil at these depths are being pushed to the limit. So we understood the pressure they were under from their customers and shareholders.

Getting these people actually to see and feel the broader scope of what Fujitsu could deliver enabled the relationship between the companies to be transformed. The company realized Fujitsu could contribute much more deeply to its business than simply fixing printers and PCs. Following this event they asked Fujitsu to change the existing relationship. They wanted to engage in broader conversations about its business so as to enable a better understanding of what value Fujitsu could deliver in supporting them.

By making the value Fujitsu could deliver more transparent to the customer, the door was opened to increasing and evolving the services being delivered. This in turn is now creating opportunities for the energy company to improve the quality and reduce the cost of its oil products both for its industrial customers and millions of motorists across the planet.

Allow them to focus on their customers

If you want to focus your employees on their customers one of the most valuable things you can do is free them from having to worry about what is happening elsewhere in your organization.

An English friend told us about his recent visit to an upmarket sushi restaurant in Miyagi Prefecture, which is a relatively rural area in northern Japan. He was the guest of his Japanese in-laws. The area is famous for its fresh fish and quality rice, all good ingredients to make perfect sushi.

The restaurant has effectively automated all the mundane aspects of its service, from order taking through to customers' payment by using state-of-the-art mobile devices. This gives the waiters and waitresses more time to make recommendations to the customers, to provide additional services and ensure that the customer enjoys the best time possible. This was particularly good for our friend's party as it consisted of 10 family members aged from 3 to 80. The grandmother in particular liked to know exactly where each fish came from and the waitress was only too pleased to indulge her.

The excellent service the party received was a consequence of how the restaurant had automated the mundane. All orders were input directly into an electronic order book which sent the order requests directly to the kitchen. This ensured that everything was absolutely fresh – particularly important for sushi when the fish could be killed just seconds before it is eaten.

In some Japanese sushi restaurants, your order arrives on little plates. The plates come in different colours, which tell you the price of the order. For example, some salmon might come on a blue plate, which costs 200 yen. The more expensive fatty-tuna might cost 600 yen and so would come on a red plate. When you have finished eating, the waitress usually stacks the plates and then works out your bill. This restaurant followed the same structure but had inserted a microchip under each plate – using technology to speed up service. This chip was then read by a scanner, which the waitress moved up each pile of plates. In seconds, the bill was calculated – all automatic and effortless. This ensures delivery is in tune with customers' needs. The system means that waitresses have no boring order-taking, or bill-totting up duties to do. Instead they can provide customers with the value-adding activities they truly appreciate – such as making recommendations and discussing the origins of the fish.

Imagine if the computers were taken away and the waitress had to calculate bills manually. It would take her time and attention to perform a task that the customer sees as a commodity (calculating a bill) and remove her from a task that the customer sees as adding value – informing them of where the fish comes from. Or, even worse, imagine that before the waitress passed an order to the chef she had to go and see him in person to convince him to do it. How much of her attention is now on providing the front-end of the service? She is still focused on the delivery, as the conversation with the chef is part of the delivery, but her need to go into the kitchen is reducing her ability to understand what her customers want and keep them satisfied, which is where her attention should be focused.

Walk in the customer's shoes to understand their tacit needs

One of the best ways to understand the customer's journey is to walk in their shoes to immerse yourself in their world. By doing this you can better understand their tacit needs and also you will begin to get in touch with the emotional aspects of their journey with greater clarity and be able to refine services to a much deeper level.

A colleague told us of a great experience he had as a result of a service provider walking in the customer's shoes. Set on a 60-acre private peninsula on the eastern coast of a tropical island in Mauritius, the Le Saint Géran Hotel offers the last word in five-star luxury hospitality services. Not only does it have rooms filled with hand-picked furniture, Egyptian cotton sheets, goose down pillows and balconies looking out on to a stretch of white sandy beach and the azure Indian Ocean, but also a Gary Player designed golf course, Givenchy treatment spa and a Michelin starred restaurant.

One thing that guests nearly always remark on is the attention to detail the hotel provides and especially how the staff are able carefully to balance their service to be attentive but never bothersome. To document all the services from the outset that the Le Saint Géran offers would be very difficult as the level of detail would be overwhelming – after all how do you capture what activity is attentive and what is bothersome? So it did not surprise our colleague to learn that the hotel had not been set up with these amazing services, but they had evolved over time. A key feature of this was allowing staff to walk in the customer's shoes.

Every month a top performing employee is rewarded with a stay at the hotel as a guest. The initiative is called FLAG day, or **F**eel **L**ike **A** **G**uest day. The employee has full use of the facilities and is treated just like a paying guest. But the difference is that while staying in the hotel they are often seen carrying a notebook, as they are encouraged to think of anything – no matter how seemingly small or inconsequential – that would help improve overall service levels for guests. What this has led to is an understanding of customers' needs to the smallest detail that simply could not be achieved in any other way.

This means that when you are lying on the beach someone is liable to come and offer to clean your sunglasses; within 24 hours all the staff know you by name and room number; when you are using the running machine in the gym, an attendant will offer you a glass of water (chilled or room temperature); and every night you benefit from aromatherapy as fragranced oils are left in your room to help you sleep. One guest forgot their contact lenses when visiting the restaurant. Without a hitch, the waiter brought a selection of prescription glasses they could borrow to read the menu!

By allowing its staff access to the customer experience, Le Saint Géran has been able to develop what many believe to be the best hotel service in the world. Gathering the information is one thing, but to provide a great service Le Saint Géran also ensures that these findings are fed through to those responsible for designing hotel services and delivering them. Le Saint Géran staff ensure that they find, explore and as far as possible eliminate the pressures and irritations of customers.

In the same way, we described in the previous chapter how Fujitsu captured Whitbread's tacit needs by having a member of the service delivery team on site at Whitbread's HQ every single day. This helped ensure that the services were supplied by someone who was in tune with

Whitbread's needs and understood the impact on the business. This helped with a myriad of service improvements, which ultimately benefited the end customer – people like us who dine in Whitbread's restaurants and stay in their hotels.

Help customers with their decision-making

With simple services customers can often reach their own decisions quite quickly. But as services become more sophisticated – and more complex – deciding what best fits you becomes more difficult. One of the key services that a provider can offer is helping customers make the right decision.

Take mobile phone services, for example. Initially the phones just made calls so the decision on which one to buy was fairly simple. It was based on the model of phone you would get (only half a dozen to choose from), price of calls and the coverage of the network. Even at this early stage it was not as easy a decision as you would think. Some providers gave cheaper calls to landlines and others to other mobiles, and then some began to offer free evening and weekend calls. So deciding what was going to be best for you required you to predict your usage of a mobile phone, which although not completely clear could be done with a fair amount of accuracy.

Now move forward 10 to 12 years and look at buying a mobile phone today. There are hundreds of different handsets available offering hundreds of different functions, and there is a massive array of tariffs offering combinations of mobile to mobile calls, mobile to landline calls, international calls, texts, picture texts, internet access, pre-pay, 3G, mobile download services, games, polyphonic ring tones, GPRS positioning and live TV. The decision of which mobile phone service to use has become exceedingly complex and is set to become more so. As a result, one of the key services a provider can offer is to help customers in deciding what is best for them. How do you do that? Well you begin by understanding the customer's journey and then show what you have to offer. The trouble is that this can create a tremendous amount of confusion for a customer.

The opposite of a feature-oriented provider – who has only one thing to offer – is the provider who will provide whatever service the customer asks for. They are completely flexible and so, on the face of it, the customer should be overjoyed. But a provider turning up with a blank sheet of paper can often be as unsatisfying for a customer as someone who has arrived with the perfect solution to their problems before they have even spoken. Too much choice can be an inconvenience.

A customer will know that they want an experience, but what they will not know is what service they should ask for to deliver that experience. A retailer, for example, might want 'all of our shop tills working all the time, with automatic updates of prices'. To help your customer to make the right decision for them, the onus is on you to make it easier for them to understand and experience your proposition.

We could, for example, be sold a car by someone showing us diagrams of how the engine is put together and works, how the transmission and exhaust systems work and (if we were still awake at this stage) diagrams of the electrical systems. The alternative is that we get into a car and go for a test drive. Very quickly we can see what works about this car for us and what does not – and it allows us to feed back valuable information that the provider can then use to make the customer experience better in the future, such as making the suspension softer. Would we have been able to provide such feedback from seeing the diagrams and charts? By giving the test drive the service provider has made our lives a lot easier and our decision-making much quicker.

Continually engage with customers

The world is changing with ever-increasing speed. Now, companies invest large amounts in developing new services that then need to change almost continually. A traditional organization with a marketing department carries out customer surveys every six months. The results of this survey decide which innovations will be invested in and which will be discarded. Such a short-sighted approach does not work in today's business world.

Let's imagine a travel agent has identified through a customer survey that many of its customers want to go to an area of the world for which they have never designed packages before. So they spend three months making arrangements for tours to be taken, hiring people, finding hotels, registering with governmental agencies and a whole host of other activities. What they did not notice was that after they had taken their snapshot customer survey the holiday country's currency had been steadily creeping up in value, making holidays to it an expensive and less attractive proposition.

A service provider delivering great service informed by continual engagement with its market would have picked up what effect this currency fluctuation was having on customer behaviour. Probably the demand for travel to this country would have dipped and so the investment would be pulled back. A snapshot taken before the currency shift began may have missed this change in demand completely.

Similarly, a great service provider continually captures knowledge and experiences from customers and prospective customers. What they cannot deliver today is just as valuable – as it drives innovation and business for tomorrow – as the information on what can be delivered. Many suppliers would simply discard this vital knowledge rather than use it to innovate new services.

Customers may tell the travel agent they want to go on safaris, a type of holiday the agent does not currently offer but *could* develop in the future. Such an approach enables continuous innovation which helps service providers to earn customers' respect and loyalty.

Take a consistent approach to the customer throughout the journey

The information captured when engaging the customer needs to be fed automatically to all the people who are involved in providing the service. Everyone involved, from selling to innovating, needs to be given the appropriate information so that they are all working to a complete picture of the customer.

A friend recounted his experience of staying at a hotel. On his first night he and his wife decided to dine at the hotel's restaurant, but he made a point of letting their waiter know that he was allergic to milk and milk-based products. On hearing this, the waiter was unable to suggest any dishes that could be made without dairy products immediately but went back to the chef to let him know of the request. A few minutes later the waiter came back with a few options that the chef could do without the use of dairy products. The couple ordered and were soon enjoying their meal.

The next day at the same restaurant the waiter approached the couple and immediately suggested which dishes could be made without dairy products – anticipating that the couple might come back that night he had already spoken to the chef. In this case the waiter fed information back through the chain to the person designing the service (the head chef) and the person delivering the service (the sous chef, who makes the dishes to the head chef's design). Over the rest of week the chef, knowing that one of his regular diners had a milk allergy, had innovated a new dairy-free dish for each day.

For the small localized service of the restaurant it was simple for staff to pass on information in face-to-face conversation and they all acted on it. For a company like Fujitsu, where tens of thousands of people are working across the globe, connecting them using a technology and then driving the behaviours to use that technology correctly by establishing a living service culture has been a challenge. Our approach to meet the challenge is to use 'templates', that help to accelerate customers' opportunities.

Agenda 3 – Engage with Customers

- ◆ Focus on understanding the customer's journey
- ◆ Help customers with their decision-making
- ◆ Continually engage with customers
- ◆ Take a consistent approach to the customer throughout the journey

CHAPTER 4

Accelerating Customers' Opportunities

In this chapter, we share the lessons we have learned in developing services that accelerate customers' opportunities. We highlight some pointers that you should bear in mind while solving customers' problems and turning them into opportunities.

We will show how 'templates' (the recipes in the baker's story) can allow us to deliver elegant simplicity. Simultaneously, we will show how to make both our own and the customers' processes transparent, in order to design collaboratively and deliver the service. Such an approach can turn problems into opportunities.

Focus on elegant simplicity

In the baker's story, we saw how Sally (solving) used simple recipes which made both her own and Des's life much easier. Because she knew how to bake a sponge, she did not need to start from scratch every morning. She also had a document containing her list of questions, the range of answers and the different cake designs that they would provide. This allowed others with Sally's levels of skill to design cake icing by simply following the steps she had designed. For Des, he could also simply follow the recipes to deliver great service to all of their customers. Sally's approach facilitated development and delivery, and was elegantly simple.

At Fujitsu, we have developed our own recipes (internally we call them *templates*) for commonly delivered services such as a service desk. A service desk logs customer problems, and then coordinates and manages the reso-lutions. For Fujitsu the service desk is the core of many of the other services provided. The service desk can be thought of as being like the sponge in Sally's cakes. Just as the sponge was at the heart of many of Sally's cakes, the service desk is at the heart of many services. And just as Sally took the time and effort to perfect her recipe for sponge so that cus-tomers were served with elegant simplicity, Fujitsu has invested in developing pre-tested templates and has used recognized international standards for designing and delivering a service desk. This ensures that all customers can now benefit from Fujitsu's optimized service desks.

One of the organizations benefiting from this is the Post Office in the UK. The Post Office is most well known as being the place to buy stamps and post mail, but over the years its role has expanded. Its 14,300 branches are visited by over 24 million customers a week who can do any-thing from validating a passport application to paying a utility bill. In fact 240 million household bills are paid at Post Offices each year, which form part of the £90 billion worth of transactions it handles every year. Fujitsu's partnership to support the Post Office stretches back to 1993. During this period 3.5 million lines of programming code have been writ-ten to create the sophisticated functionality that forms the heart of the Post Office counter systems, a highly complex solution largely developed using a traditional bespoke approach. The new service desk that supports this system, however, uses our new approach. It was pre-built and pre-tested by Fujitsu and was plugged straight into the Post Office.

Furthermore, as other templates are designed to offer additional ser-vices, they can be simply plugged into the core service desk to create an entire customer service solution for the Post Office or anyone else. This would be similar to Sally developing recipes for different icings that differ-ent customers can request to be applied to the same sponge base. With this approach, the customers' solutions become an elegantly simple collec-tion of consistent parts. Ric Francis, the operations director of the Post Office, commented on past projects, 'Fujitsu understands our business, our people and how to manage a change of this scale and complexity ... this allows us to work together to deliver a modern, reliable infrastructure that supports our branch staff in offering a better service.' We saw the application of our template approach as being a continuation of this.

Templates define prescriptive, reusable solutions. They capture the preferred process and instructions to deliver the required consistent outcome. In doing so they provide predictability in delivery, timescales, costs, skills needed and quality.

This approach also provides a number of other significant benefits. First, it is cost-effective. Sally develops her recipes only once but they make cakes for many customers. Secondly, it is reliable. Sally's recipes guarantee the taste her customers expect. Thirdly, it is simple to deliver. Sally's recipes contain enough details for anyone to make the cake. Fourthly, it takes less time to develop. Sally already has recipes developed for her cakes – she doesn't need to start from scratch each time. Finally, it allows the organization to provide more innovation and thereby provide more choice for customers. In the bakery example, a new cake developed for one customer can be sold to anyone. This makes this new development a more attractive proposition for the bakery.

In order to support a focus on elegant simplicity, we have found the following pointers are necessary for people who are accelerating customers' opportunities.

Look for standardization

We have discussed how templates (or recipes) can be used to provide a core part of a service such as a service desk for the Post Office (or a sponge base for a cake).

When accelerating customers' opportunities, as well as using such standard templates in solutions, the service developer (people like Sally) also needs continually to look out for emerging patterns within customer requirements. So the developers are not just using templates in their solutions but initiating their development too. If they find that they are developing a solution that is similar to one that they have developed several times before they need to recognize this and inform the people engaged in innovation (people like Imogen). These people will then investigate demand for this potential service to decide if this piece of work should be turned into a full template which can provide that service. In the future these templates can then be picked up by developers and plugged into a solution rather than recreated from scratch. In other words, this standardization contributes towards delivering elegant simplicity.

Often a developer will find that it is not the specific end-product service that they are developing which is similar to another but the way they are actually working. They may find that they are using a similar process from job to job to develop different templates. At this stage the developer should begin building what is called within Fujitsu a Solution Build Model (SBM). These are templates of the design processes that are followed to create solutions or parts of solutions for customers.

Each template consists of tried and tested methodologies that if a designer follows should allow them to deliver a defined output or, in other words, a standardized approach to solving standard problems. An example of this is the question and answer document Sally developed to help guide how her celebration cakes should be designed.

To demonstrate the value of the standardized approach, consider the case of Yame General Hospital in Japan. Yame Hospital is a municipal hospital serving a community of 140,000 people. Fujitsu was asked to deploy a one-stop solution to manage medical information systems and services. The solution was delivered with the use of standardized templates. Thanks to their use, the solution that was provided was low cost and could easily be kept up to date. The system contained a number of elements. The first was a comprehensive online drug prescription and administration service. There was also an X-ray and endoscope service. This service replaced doctors' handwritten notes (which were often unreadable). The new system helped to avoid errors. Also, the system made possible the sharing of information throughout the team – all the doctors and nurses could see what people had been prescribed. The patients could also see the results of the check up, see graphical representations of their medical results and be dealt with much quicker.

Apart from these benefits, the overall system resilience was increased in a number of ways. First, the total cost was lowered through the use of standardized templates which reduced operational complexity. Secondly, there was improved availability as the infrastructure had less down time and reliability increased by up to 50 per cent. Finally, as all the building blocks were extensively tested and proven to work effectively together, both implementation time and overall risk were reduced dramatically. Reduced costs and a more reliable infrastructure had clear benefits for the hospital and, more importantly, the patients. The challenge is clear: benefits such as these can be provided to any customer.

Look for scalability

Any service can be delivered in an infinite number of ways. Think of how many ways you can provide even a simple service like delivering a letter. All service providers could decide from a number of options as to how they should develop and deliver their service for their customers. The temptation is to give the customer a free hand and let them decide in great detail the service that they want to receive. But, as we have seen, such an approach can create problems for both customer and service provider.

So what option should the developers take? What should guide their approach? In simple terms they should seek to develop a service which can be used by the greatest number of customers. The service which is most scalable will provide greatest benefit to both the service provider and the customer, as the costs for developing and supporting the solution can be spread out over a greater number of customers. The customer may be offered lower costs and the service provider can invest their resources with much greater focus. As a result, the service provider can sell, solve, deliver and innovate one *great* service rather than many *adequate* services.

Look for consistency

While producing standardized and scalable templates is important, a consistent approach underpins the whole journey and is essential to delivering elegant simplicity. The knowledge flows within the service provider must be consistent throughout the sell, solve, deliver and innovate areas in order to provide a seamless service for the customer.

For example, the output from the development process is a series of documented templates that should allow a simple handover so that a service can be delivered to the customer quickly and accurately. An issue that could occur is that following the handover the delivery team begin to make changes to the design. This could be for many reasons, such as a simple customer request. As the delivery team have not been involved in the development of the solution they are unlikely to understand all the complexity in the solution produced by the developer. By making a seemingly inconsequential change at the delivery stage, the team can actually create major problems. Unforeseen relationships between what they have changed and other aspects of the service can become apparent. If, for instance, Sally were to produce a sponge which Des found to be too large for the ovens, Des may decide, without telling Sally, to reduce the size of the sponge. Such change may have an unforeseen effect as the icing production is still the same size. Now the icing is too thick for the cake and as a result the customers are not happy!

For this reason, the developers in service providers, like Sally, must remain attached to a project well into delivery and beyond so that any adjustments which need to be made can be carried out in a consistent manner. Such consistency can provide elegant simplicity.

Make processes transparent

As we have discussed, one of the key difficulties faced by many complex services is to be able to create the bridge between the customer's business and the supplier's offerings. One of the best ways to build this bridge is for both sides to work collaboratively, engaging throughout the service design process. Otherwise, many issues can arise if a customer simply supplies a brief to the service provider and then seeks to keep the relationship at arm's length. The problem is that the service provider often misunderstands the brief that has been handed over to them, and so designs something wholly inappropriate. A good service provider will often recognize any points where there is room for misunderstanding and seek clarification.

This is not always the case. The difficulty is that a brief is trying to capture the complexity and interrelatedness of the real world on a piece of paper and so will always incorporate assumptions. And assumptions can create considerable difficulties.

Imagine a very simple brief: 'I'd like a taxi, please.' In some places taxis are regulated and you know what you will get right down to the model of vehicle. But in other places, any car can be used as a taxi as long as it passes certain safety and roadworthiness tests. In these places, you have no idea what you are getting but you assume many things. Your assumptions usually include (this is not an exhaustive list) that you and whoever you are travelling with will fit into the taxi, it will be of a certain level of comfort, the driver will be in good health, it will be reliable enough to get you where you want to go, it will be fast enough to get you there in time and the driver will take the shortest or fastest route.

The other difficulty with being handed a brief is that often there are many ways of supplying the same or a similar service. Without access to the extra information that enables a service provider to choose the single most appropriate route from the many available for the customer, they will default to taking the route that is most appropriate for themselves. Imagine calling for a taxi and very carefully asking for a taxi that will take you directly from your home to Heathrow airport. Ten minutes later there is a knock on the door and you open it to see a horse-drawn carriage ready and waiting to take you to the airport. The taxi service had run out of cars so sent this instead. It will be going directly to the airport – although the horse may have to stop for water. This solution may not suit you but for now, as they have run out of cars, it suits the taxi service.

The way that a service provider can deal with these difficulties is essentially to 'show their working' or talk through their logic. Talk to the customer. Let them see the logic of your decisions so that they can question them and test the logic for themselves to see if this really is the most appropriate solution for them. If the taxi service had called you and made its process transparent by saying that they had run out of cars and so were thinking of sending a horse-drawn carriage, it would have allowed you to have an input to the solution. You could have said, 'No thanks', or you could have said, 'Fantastic – we've got lots of time before the flight leaves and what a great way to start a holiday with the kids.' Either way the solution would have evolved towards your needs, not the supplier's.

At the solve stage, therefore, a dialogue between the customer and the service provider is vital to keep the service on track and ensure that the solution fits the outcome needed, not the solution expected. There must be no surprises. The processes must be transparent on both the customer's side and the service provider's side. The only difficulty with this dialogue is when the designer is a specialist and the service that is being developed becomes too complex for the customer to understand what the designer is saying to them. This calls for designers to have excellent communication skills and tools so that they can communicate simply the complexity of what they are designing.

How can complexity be reduced by making processes transparent? We believe this can be done through the use of templates (recipes in the baker story). Think back to Sally producing her celebration cakes for customers. For a new customer, Sally would describe the cakes in terms of the sponge

and the appropriate icing – something that customers could easily understand. She would not go into the detail of all the ingredients by describing
the types of eggs, brands of flour and sources of sugar. In other words, by
aggregating information to template level you are making it far easier for
customers to understand what the entire solution being proposed is. As a
result, you ensure that the overall process is clear.

Turn problems into opportunities

Service providers need to go to the heart of customers' problems in order
to turn problems into opportunities. The trouble is that customers may
not always realize the value of the service provider's specialist knowledge
and experiences.

Traditionally, when wanting a solution, a customer may put together a
specification of features based on their understanding of the issue and
how they want it resolved. Such a specification may push the service
provider into developing a particular solution. By being so prescriptive the
solution may not include all the capabilities of the service provider and
also may not take account of elements that the customer themselves had
not realized. A far better approach would be to make the processes and
shared understanding between the customer and service provider completely transparent through continuous dialogue and knowledge sharing.
Only then can the two organizations get to the heart of the problem and
also – perhaps – produce tremendous opportunities.

An example of what can happen for a customer when they take this
step is the Spanish savings bank, Caixa d'Estalvis i Pensions de Barcelona
which is more commonly called "la Caixa". "la Caixa" is the third largest
Spanish financial institution (by assets) and the largest savings bank in
Spain. It operates from over 5,000 branches with over 25,000 employees
to serve almost 10 million clients.

"la Caixa" faced a challenge balancing its enormous local branch network with its strategy for growth and desire to improve customer services.
Its branches, in both rural and urban areas, provide a valuable service to
the local populace, but they are often run by no more than four employees. With such a limited number of employees at each branch, "la Caixa"
faced a challenge to provide its customers with the same level of service
everywhere and to grow the business.

A simple response to this problem was to propose augmenting the branches with ATMs to carry out standard transactions such as cash with-drawals and deposits, freeing up staff to serve customers with more complex needs.

As part of this initiative, Fujitsu had been working with "la Caixa" for many years providing a variety of services. In the 1980s this relationship took a major step forward when a group of senior executives from "la Caixa" visited Fujitsu in Japan and saw ATMs that used passbooks. The executives saw how Japanese bank customers, like the Spanish, preferred to have a history of their account to hand at all times. Passbooks provide such a history and so having an ATM which can update the passbook automatically was an attractive proposition. The desire of Japanese cus-tomers to retain passbooks over bank cards has meant that Japanese technology suppliers, such as Fujitsu, had developed ATMs differently to those in the west.

"la Caixa" immediately recognized that these Japanese ATMs could be a technology that fitted their customer's needs and so could help the bank move customers towards using a self service channel. The benefit for the customers would be 24-hour access to their money, while dealing with their concern of having their financial records to hand. The benefit for the savings bank would be streamlining the processes to supply this basic ser-vice so that resources could be directed towards improving value to customers in other areas.

When planning the deployment of these ATMs back in Spain, "la Caixa" considered going one step further and using the ATMs to provide other services, such as theatre, cinema and train tickets. The 24 hour ATM could be developed to provide these services. So rather than experi-encing a restricted service thanks to the limited number of staff at each branch, the customers were now receiving a greater range of quality ser-vices which mixed the best of people and technology. Fujitsu collaborated with "la Caixa" to check this idea via market research in 2002. Some 5,000 branches were surveyed and the results were positive. The research focused on not just what people wanted to do with the savings bank but more broadly what they *could* do.

The key to the savings bank's success was that, despite the pressures of the situation, it never once failed to put the needs of its customers first. "la Caixa" had the foresight to create relationships and share its challenges with a number of partners such as Fujitsu. It considered that working together with these partners, was the best way to add value to solutions. With the service providers understanding the savings bank's issues, it allowed the providers to feedback and evolve their services in line with the savings bank's needs. They then sought to offer "la Caixa" a great service so that it could offer a correspondingly great service to its customers. For "la Caixa", by having its technology supplier involved so closely, it made sure that areas of research provided solid results that allowed the best deployment of new technology which could benefit its customers. The strategy of working together with suppliers in the research, not only provided "la Caixa" with good feedback for themselves, but would assist suppliers in suggesting solutions for the improvement of its services. And for service providers like Fujitsu, to have direct access to a customer's customers allows us to understand where we should focus our efforts to provide customers with future benefits.

This approach to future development means that, as new technologies become available, "la Caixa" and its customers will demand them and pull them through. This is in sharp contrast to the traditional push model of technology suppliers, where a new technology is developed and pushed onto a market which isn't always demanding it. An example of a technology that emerged from this is a further planned improvement to the ATMs.

The new "la Caixa" ATMs validate, count and sort the money that has been deposited, so the machine requires less frequent attention to check the deposits. In turn this helps the branch staff to have more time for the customers. These machines also update account information immediately, so that you could pay in money and then, if needed, withdraw it minutes later for an emergency. This is in contrast to waiting until the next day, as with traditional ATMs that require human intervention to count money and update account information. The next step will be to enable the money deposited by one customer in the ATM to be withdrawn by someone else. This will provide even more benefits because the machine will require less frequent filling. Co-creation is cash regeneration. A business problem which is dealt with by always considering the people, technology and processes can become a great opportunity and benefit to all. The service provider, the customer and the customer's customer can all have their opportunities accelerated.

Agenda 4 – Accelerate Customers' Opportunities

- Focus on elegant simplicity
- Make processes transparent
- Turn problems into opportunities

CHAPTER 5

Delivering Great Service

Delivery is the area where the reputation of a service provider is made or unmade. Many suppliers can sell you a service; the proof of the pudding is in the delivery. This chapter develops and explains the physical functions – the processes and technology – within the delivery environment, and how they produce robust and reliable services.

One of the most important attributes of great service is that it delivers invisible excellence – you don't even think about the service you are receiving. Remember our story about going from London to Tokyo? Throughout the day many services were experienced, such as using a taxi, an ATM, check-in at the airport, the hotel's email and telephone. All the services were experienced without any fuss; they were not even noticed. Invisible excellence in action. Together with striving to deliver invisible excellence, the service provider needs to ensure that the delivery is in tune with their customer throughout the delivery process. Moreover, the service provider needs to make the delivery scalable, so that as many customers can access as many services as they require. In our bakery you can have one cake or hundreds of cakes. Des (delivering) will be able to provide you with however many you want – all with great taste and quality.

Strive to deliver invisible excellence

Customers should be able to rely on the delivery of service being so consistent that they take it for granted, like flicking a light switch to read a book or turning a tap to have a drink. The thought for the customer should not be of the electricity or water service, but of reading their book or quenching their thirst. The service should be so great that the customer does not have to give it a second thought – it has effectively dropped out of their visibility. To deliver this invisible excellence the provider needs to keep their own processes highly visible to themselves. It is only when they have complete transparency of their own processes that they can apply processes and technology to improve the quality and reduce the cost of the services – or, in other words, continually innovate the service to meet the customer's evolving needs.

As an example of a service that is continually seeking to innovate in order to provide invisible excellence, let's have a look at the story of an international airline. The company prides itself on its innovation and forward thinking. It pioneered a number of service improvements including online reservations and greater flexibility in meeting passengers' dietary requirements.

Despite these improvements, all airlines have experienced tough times in recent years due to increasing competition, heightened security concerns and deregulation worldwide. Since 2002 the need to cut costs – particularly in back-office functions such as IT – has been endemic across the industry. For our customer, this has meant a sea change in its approach to IT. The airline needed its suppliers to help reduce costs and increase efficiency.

None of this matters one jot to the airline's customers, of course. All that they are interested in is their travel experience. But how many times have you sat in a plane only to hear an announcement that there is a technical hitch? When aiming to increase efficiency, one area the airline looked at was the service desk. The desk is part of a service provided by Fujitsu for many years now and is used by the airline's employees if they have a particular IT problem – say their computer does not log on properly (we can all relate to that issue) or some other computer-related problem, which could result in a plane being delayed.

In a traditional service desk environment the customer interface is fairly impersonal and often inexpert. Problem calls are received from customers, and the service organization merely manages the flow of a call as it winds its way along the service organization. Success in such an environment is measured by the efficient management of the call (call duration, number of rings before the phone is answered etc.) and not by whether the customer's problem has been resolved – whether the aircraft leaves on time. At the airline, the major step to improving performance was to move beyond these narrow service parameters. In the improved service desk, the service desk agents were empowered to help solve the customers' problems, rather than just simply manage the call. This, in turn, helps avoid repeat calls and so eliminates waste.

The starting point was to analyze the different types of calls coming in from employees. Then, besides tracking and fixing calls, Fujitsu set to work to understand the underlying causes of the problems that were preventing the airline from delivering invisible excellence to their customers. At the same time, Fujitsu also measured the impact on the airline's business model if there was a failure or delay in resolving a call. More than half the calls were repeat complaints about recurring problems. It became apparent, for example, that some 26 per cent of the total calls were due to the malfunctioning printers used by the ground crew when printing out baggage vouchers and flight tickets. So what did this mean to the airline? It turned out that printer problems were slowing down the check-in procedure – which could ultimately cause flight delays.

Imagine if you were a passenger sitting on a delayed aircraft and you discovered that a printer caused the hold-up. You would be less than pleased. And yet, these sorts of minor, seemingly unimportant details let service organizations down all the time. But because they happen behind the scenes, the passengers remain in the dark. Not with this airline. Not any more.

It was immediately apparent that solving the printer problem was critical. Following Fujitsu's analysis, the answer the airline's management decided to invest in was better printers. As a result, the number of calls to the service desk about malfunctioning printers fell by more than 80 per cent in 18 months. This translated into major savings in flight operations, far in excess of the cost of the new printers, and, of course, far happier passengers.

In addition, the response time of technicians was improved so that the average time needed to fix printers that still failed fell from ten hours to three. This was hugely motivating for the service desk agents. Rather than simply log that there had been a printing issue, they were actually helping diagnose the issue and come up with the solution. Moreover, the agents had to speak to each other to build up a picture of what was going on. Once that picture was built, the agents had to speak with solution developers and customer engagement managers to articulate the problem. A strategy had to be agreed with the airline's management and ground staff to ensure that the delivery of the new printers was done in a way that was conducive to its business model. The success of the process relied on people. Within the service, the process of resolution became invisible. A problem was noted, logged, understood and resolved – no fuss, no bother, just great service delivered.

As a result of this success, the airline consolidated all of its IT services by awarding Fujitsu single supplier status. Fujitsu signed a 10-year out-sourcing deal with the airline covering the service desk, desktops, mid-range computers, corporate applications, voice and data networks and change management. This left the airline with an internal IT department of just 20 people (down from 128). But it is not just about numbers. Most of the airline's IT costs are variable and are now related to the real use of computer resources. This is important as one of the airline's major objectives was to ensure that IT cost levels more closely followed their usage levels. This provided greater flexibility in scaling of operations, depending on business need. Such an arrangement allows the airline to concentrate on its core business.

The contract itself played a part in the delivery of great service. Typically, one of the elements on which IT service providers are mea-sured and paid is their service desk response times to user problems, such as a malfunctioning printer. Such a model encourages both customers and service providers to reach the lowest cost possible per call handled. This call centre model gives firms no reason to reduce the number of calls received, and indeed creates a disincentive: if the call volume falls, so does the service company's revenue. Fujitsu approached the problem in a completely different way: instead of being paid for each call handled, Fujitsu asked to be paid a set fee based on the number of *potential* callers. This made it profitable to apply the successful root cause analysis, as we saw with the malfunctioning printers. Such analysis resulted in people returning to the centre of the service. Instead of profiting by people con-tinually calling with problems, Fujitsu would only benefit by delivering great service.

	March 2006	September 2007
First time fix for service desk	23.80%	58.65%
Incoming contacts	4881	3773
Outbound calls	4147	2779
Incidents logged	2671	1543
Call abandoned rate	0.23%	0.04%

TABLE 5.1 ◆ **Recent statistics showing the improvement in the running of the airline's service desk.**

So the printer problem and others have been fixed at the root cause since 2002. The result has been an ongoing continuous improvement in the service delivered by the service desk. The table above shows recent summary statistics. The airline's customers have also benefited. The chances of them suffering a delay due to an IT issue have been greatly reduced. And the reduction of a little bit of stress in an airport is good news for everyone.

Ensure delivery is in tune with the customer

A service provider should be in tune with its customers' needs when delivering a service. In the previous chapter we talked about how consistency across the service journey was of vital importance. The delivery team must never change the templates that the developers have produced. However, in order to deliver great service, it is necessary to evolve the service continually by understanding the tacit needs of the customer. Such understanding does not change the service developed but ensures that it is absolutely in tune with what the customer wants. Let us illustrate this.

A colleague of ours visited the customer help desk of a software company responsible for supporting customers across Europe. The building containing the call centre was based just south of London, so it could recruit from the steady stream of mostly young foreign students that cross the English Channel and arrive in London to improve their English.

The desk was very successful at resolving issues and scored well on all the customer satisfaction surveys that had been undertaken. It was a well-developed and well-delivered service. But, one thing stood out. Despite being developed as a standard to provide all customers with the same service, each customer was not actually receiving the same service. Why was this? Simply because each customer did not want the same service! What the desk staff had tacitly understood was that the cultural differences between the many people with different backgrounds the desk supported meant that interaction on the telephone was very different from customer to customer.

For example, a typical caller from Germany, having encountered a problem, had read the support manuals, been online to find out if their query could be answered there and then really tried everything else that they could think of before calling the help desk. The help desk for them was an absolute last resort. Once they had decided to call the desk they were impatient to get the answers they needed and the conversations were often short and businesslike, sticking to the technical matters of a solution.

A typical caller from France was very different. On encountering a problem, they would immediately call the help desk. Rarely would they have read the support manual before doing this, and it was rarer still that they had searched online. They would rather talk to someone to get the answer than read a book or look on the internet. Once on the call they would not just keep the conversation to a straightforward resolution of the problem, they would often divert off to more social conversation with the help-desk employee, building a relationship before they bothered them with the technical problem they were having.

The help desk had not been contracted to deliver this variation in service to different customers. The only variation covered in the service contract for delivery to different countries was that the help-desk operator should speak the native language of the caller, not that they should approach each call individually. But the delivery staff were tacitly refining the service they provided to create a better cultural fit with the needs of the customers calling in from across Europe.

The European help desk shows that although a service is often developed at one level – the level of technical and process needs – in its delivery it often has to deal with another level – the level of individual people with their individual tacit needs. Service becomes exemplary when the delivery is in tune with the tacit needs of individual customers.

Customer needs vary not only at the individual level. Occasionally a service will be designed that offers functionality but needs to take into account what is going on in a customer's business. Remember, for example, the story of Whitbread? The business impact of outages and failures for Whitbread was far more severe if they hit at the wrong time of the week or year. The restaurants make almost 90 per cent of their revenues on Friday and Saturday nights. An outage at the wrong time can therefore have a severe effect on their ability to deliver great customer service. Recognizing this, Fujitsu responded by giving more support to peak planning, in order to ensure that the busy times in the restaurants had a corresponding increase in the level of service cover.

Solving issues with the delivery of current services is not the only way that a deliverer can improve service for the customer. Service providers must also keep an eye out for the opportunity to offer entirely new services – complementing what they already do. Often the people involved with delivery will have the most frequent contact with customers and so have the opportunity to develop a bottom-up understanding of the customer's issues.

At Whitbread it was the people going out to fix equipment and solve issues at the various coffee shops, restaurants and hotels who had the best understanding of what Whitbread was doing to serve its customers. They also had the best chance of grasping both the difficulties and opportunities Whitbread had in delivering its day-to-day services to customers. This understanding allowed them to capture other issues that the customer was facing and report these to those responsible for continual innovation.

Make delivery scalable

One of the key features of great service is that it seeks to make delivery simple enough to make it scalable. Remember our bakery story? Des (delivering) was able to deliver any number of quality, tasty cakes and bread. Scale was not an issue – he could deliver as many cakes as their customers could eat. But how?

When delivering the cakes, Des utilized the knowledge and experience that Sally had developed as she was producing the recipes. Such was the detail in the recipes, the delivery itself was very simple. For the customers of the bakery, there were clear benefits. They could get exactly the cake they wanted, they did not need to worry about the quality of the cake, they could buy as many as they needed and they could get them delivered at lower cost.

Remember the service desk that Fujitsu delivered for the Post Office? It was built and tested from a template by Fujitsu and was plugged straight into the Post Office. As other templates were designed to offer additional services, they, too, were simply plugged into the core service desk to create an entire customer service solution for the Post Office.

Such a service desk was scalable in another way as it could also be used for another customer. And indeed it was. The same template was used to provide a service desk for a major oil company. And such was the interest sparked by this template that it contributed to Fujitsu being awarded the IT outsourcing contract from Allianz that we described in Chapter 1.

A further example where a template (the 'algorithm' in this example) was produced by an expert developer, resulting in a simple and scalable delivery, can be found in Malcolm Gladwell's bestselling book *Blink*.[1]

Gladwell describes the statistical analysis work of the cardiologist Lee Goldman in helping doctors to make decisions on what to do with heart attack victims in an accident and emergency department. In the 1970s, Goldman fed the details of hundreds of heart attack cases into a computer, looking at what sort of things actually predicted a heart attack. In so doing, he came up with an algorithm which he believed could take the guesswork out of treating chest pain.

From his algorithm, Goldman proposed that as well as using the evidence of the electrocardiogram (ECG), doctors should ask specific questions – such as 'Is there fluid in the patient's lungs?' and 'Is the patient's systolic blood pressure under 100?' From these questions a decision tree could then be constructed. Following this tree through could guide the doctor on what treatment should be provided. This compared with the standard process by which a doctor would make a diagnosis on the basis of the ECG result and their own professional prognosis alone.

Gladwell then goes on to describe how the algorithm was tested in a Chicago hospital and proved to be 70 per cent better than the system reliant on a doctor's own expertise. The benefits for the hospital were immense. For the patients, it meant that those who were in need of treatment could be treated straightaway by the available doctors rather than have to wait for specialist cardiologists, and those who were not actually suffering from a heart attack would not take up much needed bed space in the hospital – and could be quickly reassured. A bed in the intensive coronary unit was costing around $2,000 a night, so there were clear financial benefits for the hospital.

The story indicates how an intense, well-thought-out, developed solution can reduce complexity on the delivery front line. This solution was both simple and scalable for use in other hospitals.

Agenda 5 – Deliver Great Service

◆ Strive to deliver invisible excellence

◆ Ensure delivery is in tune with the customer

◆ Make delivery scalable

CHAPTER 6

Co-creating the Future

I n 1994, the management thought leader, C.K. Prahalad, co-authored *Competing for the Future*,[1] with Gary Hamel. The book introduced the phrase 'core competencies' into the business lexicon. In his recent book (written with Venkat Ramaswamy), *The Future of Competition* (2003),[2] Prahalad argues that globalization and the internet have changed the rules of the competitive game. Customers are no longer abstractions that have to be satisfied, instead they are a more powerful and proactive figure. The concept of value has also changed. It is not inherent in products or services. It cannot be instilled by producers or providers. It has to be co-created with customers. Through understanding and experience, this journey is travelled together. It is from this journey that true innovation occurs. As a director of a Fujitsu customer, a global media company, told us, 'If it's not helping [our organization] satisfy more customers, gain more business, grow our revenue or improve our profitability why would we bother with innovation?'

Innovation, however, should not limit itself to developing offerings for customers. Continual innovation is also needed within the service provider to enable its own operations to evolve. The people responsible for innovating should not only be looking for new services and new markets, but should also be driving strategic activities ranging from sell, solve, deliver to innovate. In this way these people are not just looking at what customers want from the service provider – improving services to current customers – but are also helping define which customers the service provider wants to serve in the future. They respond to strategic intent provided by senior management, to drive the organization's journey into the future.

We believe that to innovate successfully the service provider must continually collaborate with its customers through multiple points of contact. The service provider also needs to recognize that innovation can come from anyone, anywhere, at any time. This means involving everyone in the journey. It is particularly important that people involved in innovation build relationships with those who are engaging with customers to test and promote new ideas. Finally, it is vital to recognize that no organization is an island. Rather, it is part of the wider business ecosystem that extends to a network of customers, partners and suppliers. In the future, it will be increasingly important to recognize this fact and co-evolve within the ecosystem.

Continually collaborate with the customer

One of the failings of traditional service is its inability to adapt to unpredicted future trends and changing customer demands. Worse, sometimes customers discover they are not protected from even predictable changes in the services they are receiving – such as legislative and technological changes.

The ability of a service provider to innovate with customers is largely controlled by the people responsible for engaging with customers. As an example let's look at how the major UK retailer WH Smith's attitude to innovation has changed.

In a typical year around 70 per cent of the UK's population visit WH Smith's 543 high street stores and 259 travel outlets, buying over 40 million books and over 75 million magazines. Its 17,000 staff serve over 1.2 million people a day.

Competitive pressure in retail has been constant and vigorous in recent years. Customers have become increasingly demanding in both the range of books and magazines they want to read and the level of service they expect. WH Smith's position as one of the UK's favourite stores has also been challenged by new competitors. Internet retailers offer convenience, and have virtually no limitation on their volume of stock. New high street book stores offer a wider range of books, and even supermarkets now offer bestsellers at discount prices.

WH Smith has always reviewed and evolved its retail offering to meet the needs of its customers, proven by its ability to trade successfully for over 216 years. But rarely in its long history have its customers' needs and competitive environment changed so rapidly and dramatically. The company realized that the changing shopping habits of customers and continuing innovations, from both on-line and physical retailers, would not subside. To meet this set of new challenges WH Smith focussed itself to increase its understanding of its customers and seek innovative ways to deliver outstanding service.

As a result, WH Smith has gone through a series of transformations, with its suppliers, to foster greater innovative thinking. For example, in addition to ensuring it has a competitive on-line presence, WH Smith is focussing business development towards new locations to suit its customers, acquiring more travel and specialist sites, such as train stations, motorway services and airports. Such sites often intensify the challenges that are faced by all WH Smith stores. Floor space is often more limited, forcing tough decisions about the ratio of shelf space, to offer the range customers want and service space, to ensure that they are served promptly and correctly. The demand at these sites can also vary more, both across the day, and by time of year.

To meet these challenges and deliver the best services to customers, WH Smith is demanding that partners offer new innovations, especially at new prestige sites such as the recently won concessions at Heathrow's new Terminal 5, set to become one of Europe's busiest retail environments.

Fujitsu's continual collaboration with WH Smith has opened new opportunities for both companies. Our team responsible for engaging with WH Smith is continually seeking to understand WH Smith's customers' changing needs, which allows the team to really understand WH Smith's business drivers. Discussions cover all business areas. To support this, every month a high level 'Points of View' document is sent to senior managers at WH Smith discussing new developments within and outside of IT which may impact on the retail sector. This is used to generate ideas and dialogue between the companies.

The early results of these initiatives are promising. WH Smiths' staff have already attended innovation days, where they get their hands-on relevant technologies and decide which to trial in their stores. Two such innovations have gone on to successful trials: the Fujitsu B-pad and the Irisys queue management system.

The B-pad is a hand held computer, (similar to a large PDA) that can be loaded with a variety of applications to do many different tasks. It can operate as a till or a stock scanner, provide immediate access to on-line systems such as stock and price files, and can run other customer service applications. It is small, light and robust. Yet it contains the latest technologies, including wireless communications to process payments, and update live financial and stock records.

At WH Smith the B-pad has been loaded with a version of the system used to operate the company's fixed tills. On noticing queues are getting long, store staff can take their B-pads out to customers and process cash and card transactions in real-time on the retail floor, even providing a receipt via a small printer attached to their belts. This lets the assistant go to the customer, rather than the customer having to come and queue at the cash desk. This shows the retailer's customers that the company is putting them at the centre of everything. It reduces the length of queues and gives the company greater flexibility in how valuable floor space is used.

But the B-pad does more than offering a mobile point-of-sale. When queues are short it doesn't simply sit in the store room gathering dust. Instead it can be loaded with other applications to allow it to do other activities that help WH Smith deliver an excellent service. It can become a stock scanner so that staff can take the same device but now use it to carry out a stock check. The B-pad's wireless capability can allow it to update a central stock database or re-ordering system in real-time, or as a mobile printer for printing stock labels.

Another offering that has emerged from the new relationship is from the Irisys system, brought to WH Smith's attention by Fujitsu. This monitors queues, footfall and movement through stores so that staff can be placed where they can serve their customers better, be it on a till, on the shop-floor with a B-pad or bringing in new stock from the back. As these innovations go live there will be more staff in the right places, equipped to assist customers with what they want, be it a quick purchase before their train departs or a search of the complete stock for a particular item.

There are three additional elements that we have found can help enable continual collaboration with customers. These are anticipating change that will affect customers, helping them bridge the gap between today and tomorrow and establishing customer experience centres.

Anticipate change that will affect customers

A condition for ensuring that innovation remains aligned with customers' needs is anticipating change and understanding the impact this has on a customer's business. In this regard, a mindset which is prepared to foster continual innovation is invaluable.

Let's take the changing data storage needs required today as an example. The data storage space required by organizations has been growing rapidly recently. It is becoming increasingly important to keep data because of increased legislation and for general auditing purposes. All this data must be kept for a certain period so that it can be analyzed when necessary. The amount of data that organizations store has been growing continuously and, therefore, a large storage space is required. Nowhere is this more critical than with professional services firms, which have to store financial data and records for their clients.

Previously, in conventional services, firms had to estimate how much storage space they would require for four or five years and then invest in the appropriate amount of storage and facilities. However, it has been getting more and more difficult to estimate how much space is required, and also as the requirements for storage space are forever increasing, the investment requirement has become a huge burden.

In an age of information overload, the need of organizations for more and more data storage is getting out of control. Traditional models of in-house and outsourced solutions are proving expensive simply because they are never able to forecast how much storage would be required in the future. 'Why', people have asked, 'can't storage be just like another commodity such as electricity where you pay when you need it?' The request is for a storage solution that can expand with demand, but with individual organizations paying only for what they actually use. This is the need; can such a service be delivered?

Such a model is difficult to produce, but a team consisting of people from Fujitsu in the UK and Japan came up with an innovative approach which is meeting the storage needs of many organizations. The new approach has completely rewritten the book for how storage can be delivered to organizations. Soon organizations will be able to use data storage on demand, just as we use electricity or water today. In this service, organizations will access IT resources in a similar way, and that is why we call it a 'utility' IT service. They will be able to request the increase or decrease of the required storage at any time.

This service can offer many benefits to customers. First, they do not now have to make an initial investment in a large storage facility or servers by themselves. Secondly, the ongoing cost is cheaper when compared with the in-house managed service – it is after all costly to hold and maintain the large data storage and the facilities in anticipation of future expansion and requirements. Finally, they do not need to worry about the maintenance and ongoing administration for the storage and facilities, as Fujitsu will take care of these.

What we see is a service that provides the customer with invisible excellence. Customers do not have to worry what is happening in the background of the service – the service provider keeps planning the optimum facility investment. It estimates when and how much the data storage space is needed, by considering the customer's business status and the industry trends. It also maintains the robust and resilient environment which can adapt and evolve to the needs and growth of the customer.

Help customers bridge the gap between today and tomorrow

In the short term, new innovations can sometimes create as many problems for a customer as they solve. This is because in order to move from the customer's current state to their new desired state requires change. And change is often a painful process. The service provider must seek to assist customers with these change processes.

A great service provider will enable a customer to visualize clearly what their service will look like after the change. This removes any uncertainty for the customer and allows a collaborative management of the change. The other advantage for the customer is peace of mind. They know that once they get to the end-state, the new service will work. This was not always the case. In the past, many customers found that after taking the time and expense to change the way they worked in order to access the new service, the service did not deliver.

When the service provider is collaborating with the customer to provide new innovations, the provider needs to take into account the customer's current state as well as their future direction. This is so that the innovations that are offered to customers do not require them to take too large or too risky a leap. The service provider needs to be wary that it understands clearly its customer's current situation, so that it develops and offers innovations that customers are actually in a position to accept.

Provide opportunities for interactive customer experience

In order really to understand what customers want, Fujitsu holds a variety of activities. These activities take many different forms. Customer experience centres, for example, are an opportunity for a customer to experience new services so they can assess them for their appropriateness. In a flexible and secure environment, the centre helps the customer learn how the service can work for them (see Figure 6.1).

There can even be virtual demonstrations such as a web conferencing demonstration made as part of a unified communications demo. Given the kind of technology being demonstrated, a virtual demo makes sense for this particular situation. Many customers understand the benefits of demonstrating their wares in front of their customers. For example, London's famous toyshop, Hamleys, gives active demonstrations of new toys to all its customers. The demonstrators are especially good at interacting with children and explaining things in an easy to understand manner – as you would expect in a toyshop!

Other activities include breakfast briefings and 'CIO connect' events. While Fujitsu might start off these meetings with a broad explanation of the

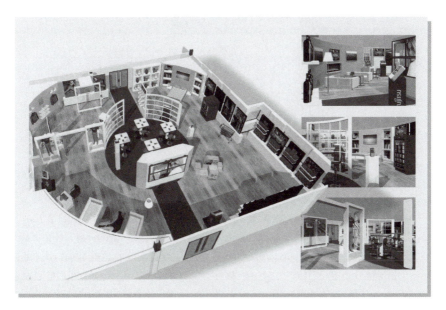

FIGURE 6.1 ◆ **An example of a customer experience centre (retail)**

service, the intimate atmosphere (only a handful of customers attend at any one time) enables us really to understand how the customers are reacting to the proposition in front of them. By capturing the tacit dimension – the feedback from the audience – the explanation can be tailored to match what the customers actually need. All in all, it is an opportunity to listen to what the customers *really* need, rather than telling them what we *think* they need.

One of the challenges service providers may meet when seeking a collaborative approach is that customers have so often in the past received dying services that many have developed a habitual behaviour to keep suppliers at arm's length. So a final activity that a service provider must undertake when setting off on the journey is to share their new approach passionately with customers. They must demonstrate their own commitment, and the benefits of forming a relationship that will provide a truly great service for the customer.

Enable all to contribute to the customer's journey

The Body is energized by flows of knowledge initiated by the needs of customers. This means that the people involved with innovation take ideas and input from anyone. To achieve this it is necessary for the various innovation processes to be transparent to all. This compels continual innovation at every level of the service, from the strategic inputs used to design the overall service to low-level service delivery. New customer needs could be discovered by anyone in sell, solve, deliver or innovate. This is an important point because it is often the people who are closest to the customer (sell) that are best able to explain how an innovation fits their needs. Those who are engaging with customers are also best placed to test the new innovations with the customers.

For example, imagine you are a late nineteenth-century stockbroker and you are approached by an inventor who offers you the following:

An arrangement of capacitors and resistors with a built-in sound mechanism activated by a high voltage pulsating signal which when attended to by the user disconnects via a switch-hook the sound mechanism and connects an electrical circuit containing a transmitter with a variable electric current which changes in response to a variable resistance device activated by acoustic pressure waves. This variable current can then be carried by a copper conduit to another similar device containing a small electrical coil which creates a flux in magnetic field to enable a physical movement of a diaphragm device which in turn creates acoustic pressure waves of a similar pattern to those input at the first device.

Interested? What if someone told you instead: 'It will allow you to talk to people at all your major trading floors, so you can react more quickly to market changes and make you thousands of dollars a month. It costs just $10. We call it a telephone would you like it?' Just imagine if Alexander Graham Bell had given up on the telephone because he had given only a technical explanation and no one could understand how they could make money from it.

Additionally, the people in innovation must also work with the people in solve and deliver. Remember the baker's children. Imogen (innovating) worked closely with Stuart (selling), Sally (solving), and Des (delivering). Imogen helped Sally, for example, by finding new ingredients for her recipes – but Sally also helped Imogen by telling her how the new ingredients could lead to new recipes. Imogen could then ask Stuart if he could sell those recipes.

Everyone can innovate and the people involved with innovation should encourage this by bringing people together around a particular customer problem or new technology. The innovation area provides the global processes and frameworks that enable others to innovate.

For example, Toyota brings people from all over the company together every month for the two years before a car goes into production, typically from design, manufacturing, logistics, marketing and sales. They discuss everything openly and share their ideas. 'It's a cross functional approach. It's about creating more communication between the people in those divisions so that they can do their jobs better', says Don Esmond, senior vice president and a general manager at Toyota Motor Sales USA. 'There are no taboos in the new, open office. Everyone in that room is an expert. They all have a part to play in building the car. With everyone being equally important to the process, we don't confine ourselves to just one way of thinking our way out of a problem', explains the chief engineer of the Corolla. As a result of this new approach, the market performance of Corolla increased by more than 10 per cent.

Co-evolve with your business partners and suppliers

It is vital to recognize that no organization exists in isolation. Each organization is part of the wider business ecosystem that includes customers, partners and suppliers. To thrive in this ecosystem, organizations need to collaborate with others in a whole range of areas.

A service provider will also often have access to advanced knowledge in their specialist field. This can be shared with customers to assist them in creating a future roadmap. This process of sharing can also benefit the service provider in refining their own roadmap for future services. Fujitsu, for example, invests significant resources in research and development (R&D). The key focus is on creating value-added solutions that leverage and combine our wide range of cutting-edge technologies in IT services, computers, networks, electronic devices and other relevant areas. More than 14,000 development engineers and 1,500 research scientists work for Fujitsu as part of R&D activities, collaborating with many leading research institutes throughout the world. This investment in R&D also enables us to extensively pre-test and pre-validate our new developments, before implementing them to deliver great service for our customers and their customers. This means that we can offer customers reliable services that deliver invisible excellence. By sharing this wealth of research with our customers, not only are they able to update their own roadmaps that they can expect in our services but also Fujitsu can get early feedback which drives the direction of our own development.

Relationships with other organizations – partners and suppliers – also play an important role. When a customer has a relationship with a service provider they should also be able to plug into the service provider's networks. For example, Fujitsu's relationships with partners such as Microsoft, SAP and Oracle are equally as important for many of our customers as our own R&D.

An alliance with Microsoft was founded on the basis that Fujitsu has strength in providing managed services and Microsoft has strength in providing software that can help run companies (otherwise known as enterprise applications). By working together, the strengths of both sides can be advanced for the benefit of our customers. A Microsoft practice has been built within Fujitsu that is looking to leverage the best in the two companies' joint expertise. This is done by creating pre-tested standardized service templates using a combination of Fujitsu and Microsoft technologies. These allow the speedy, reliable and cost-effective roll-out of Microsoft-based solutions which have benefited customers in a number of areas.

Taken together, the organic R&D and our various alliances provide Fujitsu with a strong basis to keep our customers ahead of the game continually. Running in tandem with this are processes to channel the innovated products quickly into new templates which will make up future services. Moreover, as already indicated, these processes allow feedback from the sell, solve and delivery areas to provide focus or issue resolution for the innovation area to resolve. Such continual two-way dialogue between the supplier and the customer ensures that the evolving business needs of the customer are never forgotten.

Another collaboration that has allowed innovation to occur involves an international airline, where we have established a process that proactively captures their evolving needs, called the 'Innovation hour'. The idea is that, once a fortnight, Fujitsu's account manager meets the airline's CIO and one or two appropriate managers to discuss a particular issue. The managers from both companies are drawn from the area of the business where this fortnight's chosen issue is located. The aim of the meeting is to cut through bureaucracy and focus on a highly specific issue. At the meeting people throw in new ideas and come up with innovative solutions for the most pressing problems. Some issues, because of their longevity and intractability, become omnipresent within a service process and are not solved directly. Instead they become a minefield to navigate around. By using the time in the Innovation hour to focus on such issues, long-lasting and enduring service productivity improvements are achieved.

As the airline's business model evolves and new challenges emerge, so the service will adapt to keep up. Just as the old record shop owner we mentioned in the Introduction provided a service by recommending music to his customers, we are providing a service which allows the airline to concentrate on its core business of flying passengers around the world.

Other service providers may be innovating in other areas well away from IT. But the principles articulated here are universal. That is to say, in order to be successful a company needs to be aware and ahead of current market trends, to synthesize evolving customer needs and then collaboratively provide appropriate services to meet those needs by co-evolving with partners and suppliers.

Agenda 6 – Co-create the Future

- Continually collaborate with the customer
- Enable all to contribute to the customer's journey
- Co-evolve with your partners and suppliers

PART 3

Soul 魂 Tamashii

In human beings, the soul is the inner essence that guides the mind and body. It is the energy that keeps us going; informs our conscience; helps manage the quality and characteristics of life – where we stand on important issues; and is our essential humanity.

In much the same way, people are the Soul of organizations. So harnessing the collective energy and creativity of people is one of the most important elements for living service. The Soul is inextricably linked with both the Mind – receiving strategic direction – and the Body – working with the physical framework.

Soul is not only about the moment. It is about utilizing the models and tools we have discussed in order to secure a sustainable future for us all.

CHAPTER 7

Maximizing Collective Energy

I *t was on a dreary night of November that I beheld the accomplishment of my toils. With an anxiety that almost amounted to agony, I collected the instruments of life around me that I might infuse a spark of being into the lifeless thing that lay at my feet. It was already one in the morning; the rain pattered dismally against the panes, and my candle was nearly burnt out, when, by the glimmer of the half-extinguished light, I saw the dull yellow eye of the creature open; it breathed hard, and a convulsive motion agitated its limbs.[1]*

So begins Chapter 5 of Mary Shelley's classic, *Frankenstein*, the story of Dr Victor Frankenstein who creates a living body from an assembly of body parts collected from the recently deceased. Putting the parts together was not enough to 'infuse a spark of being' – to give the creature life. Frankenstein's creation was not naturally a living body; it required an impulse of electricity in order to come to life.

In many ways the traditional structures of business organizations are similar to Frankenstein's monster. They rely on created impulses, such as the ideas of individuals and initiatives to design new improved processes, to operate. An impulse may be someone in sales deciding that it is a good idea to tell R&D something that they heard at a customer meeting, or someone in R&D deciding to tell sales of a project they are thinking of developing and setting up a process that will allow sales to see what is coming down the development pipeline and possibly even get their input. Typically this is how organizations begin to set up processes actually to get things done. The success of these processes is a major factor in enabling the organization to deliver living service.

Traditional organizations face many challenges. One of the most common is that, despite senior management setting up a general direction with an organizational strategy, the lack of definition of the relationships between the different parts of the organization leads to different interpretations and departments working at odds with one another. For example, senior managers declare a need to get closer to customers, so the IT function decides that it will give everyone in the company a common set of programs on their PCs, as this will allow everyone to communicate better and so share customer issues more effectively. However, unbeknown to IT, the sales function has decided to use an application that allows the sales force to get closer to customers, but the information cannot be shared with the new application being promoted by IT.

The same general direction provided by strategy has been acted on by different parts of the organization – but together they do not add up. As a result, the organization staggers along like Frankenstein's monster, with the different body parts moving in different directions. Could it be corrected? Yes, usually by formalizing the relationship between the departments and passing an edict, such as no new applications are to be installed without the agreement of IT. Sales may not be happy – after all, their application might have added more business value than the connectedness that IT is seeking to deliver, but at least the situation would be resolved.

The bigger problem with this way of organizing is that there is nothing inherent in the organization that makes it live: individuals who have ideas for improvements and then act on them provide the life. They create the bolts of electricity that can bring the dead corporate body to life. This is not inherently bad. It is always people who ultimately get things done. But placing such a big responsibility on individuals creates a lot of pressure for companies to spend time and money to find, develop and retain the people who can create these pulses of life.

What is the alternative? How can we create a living corporate body to deliver living service rather than rely on one being developed piecemeal? Companies can learn a lesson from life itself. Life is a tremendously successful organizing force. But to create such an organic business requires more than simply stitching some business functions together and hooking it up to a power source. It requires a Soul.

A wise man once said, 'the beat of your heart is the rhythm of your soul'.

In this chapter we will look into the Soul – the people and culture (DNA) elements of an organization. Too many organizations have proclaimed the importance of people and then treated them like disposable parts in a machine. That is a great shame. But not everyone is so cynical.

A director from a leading global payment organization observed: 'Unleashing the human potential to me is what [innovation and success] is all about. It is not about technology or a standard. It is about having the right person, in the right place doing the right thing.'

In her book, *Living Strategy*, Professor Lynda Gratton of London Business School sought to demonstrate that it is indeed people, not finance or technology, who lie at the root of sustained competitive advantage for organizations.[2] She puts forward three central tenets that differentiate people from the other elements within the organization and uses these to explain why human capital should be put at the centre of corporate strategy. These tenets are:

◆ *People operate in time* – people's behaviour is influenced by the past and by their beliefs about what will happen in the future. People working together go through a shared sequence of skills and knowledge which may take years to develop. Such knowledge shapes attitudes and values. It is important that those values are in tune with corporate strategy and processes to exploit collective energy.

◆ *People search for meaning* – people strive to understand their role and interpret the messages, both explicit and tacit, given out by the organization. This helps them understand what they as individuals can contribute to the business. Over time, groups of people create collective viewpoints as well as knowledge, which help to give them meaning about their role within the organization. Within living service, this refers to the interaction between the Mind and the Soul – people receiving strategic direction.

◆ *People have a soul* – people's energy plays a part in their working lives. They may or may not feel committed and inspired, and in turn they may give or withhold their knowledge and energy.

It is people who respond to the strategic direction of the Mind and manage the process flows we encountered in the Body section. It is people who can adapt and evolve to the customer's needs, and finally it is people alone who can really understand, honour and respond to the Mind-Body-Soul of the customer.

Living service is a synthesis of the science of processes and the art of people. No matter how good the process and technology, they need people to use them.

Let us consider how we can maximize people's energy to get the best out of them. The principal way this happens is by providing people with the time and space to allow their contribution to be fully realized. Effectively, people must be given the chance to explore the organization in which they work in order to reach their innovative potential.

Ensure people can realize their own and their customers' dreams

The strategic direction of a company and the processes within it must be aligned to allow people actively to create and continuously improve the services which are offered to customers.

An example of this occurred in Japan in the 1950s. Toshio Ikeda (1923–74) was a former Fujitsu senior executive, and said to be the pioneer of computer development in Japan.

Born in Tokyo in 1923, by all accounts Ikeda was a remarkable individual. When young he excelled at mathematics. One day, using his maths skills while playing the Japanese board game Go, he pointed out some defects in the rules. As a result, most of these defects have been remedied in the current official rules. He was one of those passionate individuals who just never seemed to give up.

He joined Fuji Communications Equipment Manufacturing Co. (the precursor of Fujitsu) in 1946 after the Second World War ended. At that time the Nippon Telegraph and Telephone Public Corporation (now known as NTT) used Fujitsu communications equipment. As a result of this contract, it became one of Fujitsu's bestselling products. Much to management's consternation, however, a problem was found with the dial operation of the phone. In one of his first tasks for the company, Ikeda was asked to look into the problem. He analyzed the operation of the dialling mechanism and helped to find the root cause. His management took notice.

In the 1950s, Fujitsu pursued the development and manufacture of computers. While the driving force behind this development was Ikeda, he received vital support from Taiyu Kobayashi. Kobayashi, Ikeda and their team thought Fujitsu could develop a relay-type automatic computing machine by making use of the company's experience in relay technology used in telephone exchanges.

At the same time, Fujitsu was asked to develop a stock dealing settlement computing machine for the Tokyo Stock Exchange. Fujitsu management saw this as a potential stepping stone for the development of their computers. Ikeda and others set to work under the management of Kobayashi.

Ikeda was an extraordinary character. When he was in one of his creative moods, he would focus strongly on a subject and forget about everything else – so much so, that he would sometimes forget to go into the office! Kobayashi understood Ikeda's talent and supported him so that he could perform to the best of his ability. For example, at that time Fujitsu's salary system was based on daily attendance. If you did not come to the office, your salary was deducted for that day. Because of his approach to work, Ikeda sometimes did not get any salary or bonus. Kobayashi and Ikeda's colleagues spoke on his behalf and the company agreed to pay Ikeda a fixed monthly salary as an exception.

Ikeda and his colleagues completed the development of a stock dealing settlement computing machine in 1953. This inspired the development of a relay-type automatic computing machine which succeeded it. The FACOM 100 was completed in 1954. It was Japan's first practical scientific computer. The FACOM 100 could complete scientific and engineering calculations much faster than traditional manual processing. It responded to multiple integration questions presented by Hideki Yukawa – a Japanese theoretical physicist and the first Japanese person to win a Nobel Prize – calculating the perfect solution in just three days. If manually computed, it would have taken two years to come up with the answer. Fujitsu was subsequently inundated with interest in the FACOM 100.

It is easy to see how the foresight of Ikeda and Kobayashi contributed to the computer revolution which Fujitsu helped pioneer. Through Kobayashi's support, Ikeda helped spark the computing revolution which has affected us all. Helped further by the company's willingness to adapt its practices, Ikeda was able to maximize his potential. In time, that potential allowed countless others – users of computers, like you and me – to make the most of their talents, too.

In order to ensure people can realize their dreams, we believe two further elements – allowing champions of change to lead and having an igniting purpose – are also necessary.

Allow champions of change to lead

There are times when a champion of change is required to challenge the status quo. Such champions can reshape the corporate environment as they question received wisdom and assumptions in their efforts to get closer to the needs and requirements of the customer. Remember the role of Bill Simpson, the account director for Reuters. He and Reuters CIO, David Lister, were instrumental in strengthening the relationship between the two companies.

The first step was ensuring that Fujitsu could deliver what Reuters truly required. The seeds of this were sown during the office move to Canary Wharf. The success of this project led ultimately to the handling of all their global IT. The Reuters vision was to reduce costs and improve productivity by simplifying its IT infrastructure and so have fewer incidents requiring less resources. The issue from a Fujitsu perspective was that we needed to further extend our global delivery model. Without such a model, the company would fall at the first hurdle. The vision would not be fulfilled.

Simpson and his team responded to Reuters by demonstrating how Fujitsu would integrate best-of-breed IT delivery partners around the world, offering a compelling Global Operating Model. In August 2007, Reuters and Fujitsu signed a global outsourcing deal with a value of £500 million over the next 10 years.

So how was this contract won? There are two lessons to learn. First, a champion of change, supported by the team, was given the scope to challenge the status quo of existing models. Had Reuters sought such an IT partner a few years ago, the old Fujitsu might not have been able to respond. However, rather than try to create a single supplier system, Simpson's team focussed on Fujitsu being a 'global aggregator' to deliver services to Reuters. This model ultimately played to Fujitsu's strengths and resulted in a solution that fitted Reuters needs.

Secondly, a successful bid required joined up and strong teamwork not just within Fujitsu but also with its partners. In this, Simpson was instrumental in breaking down silos and establishing a harmonious relationship for all people inside and outside of Fujitsu. Many different Fujitsu departments were involved with the bid. All had to step up to the mark for the bid to be successful. Various application and infrastructure teams contributed to the solution design. The commercial and financial team not only worked out the costs but were hugely innovative in structuring a deal that supported both Fujitsu and Reuters financial needs. Ancillary services were provided by legal, sourcing and marketing. The significant people aspects were dealt with by the human resources team, who had to work out how to transfer staff in 40 countries. Also, partners such as Dell, Satyam and SBS needed to work seamlessly for the customer. To produce a holistic service, the contribution of many different brains was required. Behind any success the first step must always be to break through corporate silos to maximize the contribution of all.

An igniting purpose

'An igniting purpose', according to Lynda Gratton in her book *Hot Spots*, 'can be a vision, question or task'. The igniting purpose is something 'that people find exciting and interesting and worth engaging with'.[3] In other words, people want to become part of a movement.

A spark that creates a purpose can inspire people to seek new ways of working with customers. New opportunities and new ideas can flow into reshaping the strategy and processes within the company. This can help and evolve relations with the customer. All of the attributes of living service – being people-centred, elegantly simple, adaptability and so on – require fresh ideas to keep them relevant.

As an example of an igniting purpose consider how Fujitsu re-energized its services to the retail sector, supplying services to major retailers. In 2004 Mark Dorgan (now the European Retail Partner with the company and head of the global Customer Experience Offer Platform programme) was asked to develop a new strategy for the retail sector. This simple request kick started a chain of events which has fundamentally reshaped the way Fujitsu deals with potential customers.

The starting point for Dorgan was to truly listen to retail customers. Customers valued working with suppliers who were prepared to listen and learn about their business challenges. Next, they insisted that their supplier must understand their customers in order for the relationship to be a success. This is particularly important in the highly competitive and fast moving retail world. Finally, they wanted a supplier who could help simplify things for them in terms of processes and technology.

Dorgan started by recruiting internally and externally people from retail consulting and specialist backgrounds so they could engage with customers at a business level, not just an IT level and build a renewed, integrated retail IT services offer that could deliver 'simple solutions in a complex world'. This included mobilizing people across Fujitsu, to collaborate, share expertise and deliver value-added solutions. This also meant that Fujitsu was able to understand and engage with customers at many levels. Instead of simply dealing with the IT director only, more doors were opened. This enabled much better understanding of the customer's strategy and processes. Collective energy began to build, supported by a renewed and cutting edge solution set.

Dorgan then refocused the organization on consumer trends, both via analysts and through consumer research. The original igniting purpose was now encouraging us to consider the customers' customers as well as the customers themselves. We knew that consumers like choice, value, convenience and simplicity. We began to delve into this further to understand particularly how technology – the services that the company could offer – could impact on the future retail experience.

One of the areas of research, for example, was consumer attitudes towards self service. What do people really think about the kiosks we see in railway stations which allow us to buy tickets or in airports which allow us to check in? We found that most people, even older people, are surprisingly keen on such kiosks. They help extend choice, convenience and simplicity and so have a part to play within the consumer's retail experience.

This increasing range of dialogues means Fujitsu is now proactively engaging with customers – previously we just responded to requests for information. These dialogues enable a much greater understanding of the customer's complete lifecycle and help map the overall customer journey. This in turn enabled Fujitsu to understand more clearly what services it could provide and how it could add value to the customer's people, processes and technology and therefore business success.

A good example of this is what happened at Vodafone Retail (a leading mobile phone provider). Vodafone redesigned its stores to maximize the customer experience, based on research to identify customer insights.

New technology – such as the award winning queue management system 'Q-MATIC', installed and maintained by Fujitsu – is helping Vodafone serve its retail customers more effectively.

Such knowledge can now be leveraged across the retail sector – from grocery stores to department stores and DIY. The upshot is that Fujitsu is able to provide retail customers with a toolkit of solutions that deliver a seamless brand experience. This is done by understanding how to maximize the customer's capabilities for their customers. Traditionally a shop's customer may have only been able to buy from a shop via the cash register. Now they have opportunities to utilize the internet, self-service, contact centres and so on, even in the store. With the right strategy, a retailer can use all these technologies to enhance the overall customer experience.

From one igniting purpose, Dorgan has managed to foster a whole new way of thinking and acting within Fujitsu. By adopting a consultative listening approach and embarking on consumer research, a fundamental shift has taken place, from commodity IT supplier, to thought leader in customer experience. Fujitsu is now building the Customer Experience Platform of the future – the approach is also shaping the use of the technology itself. Along the way, energy has been maximized across the supplier, the customer and most importantly the customer's customer.

All this has been reflected in the results. In the first year of the new strategy Fujitsu more than doubled its business in the retail sector in continental Europe and in 2007 the company was voted by the industry as the European Retail IT Supplier of the Year.

The experience of transforming the Fujitsu approach in the retail sector has served as a hot-house for refining the way Fujitsu works with customers and is now being replicated in each other sector by turn.

Break organizational silos

Another way in which innovation can be unlocked is through the organizational structure of a company. This has been pioneered by Toyota within the much vaunted Toyota Production System. One key component of the system is its acceptance of a level of fluidity in organizational structure. Consider for example Toyota's engine-machine plant in Kamigo in Japan. The plant has two machine divisions, each of which has three independent production shops. In the first division, the production people answered to shop heads and the process engineers answered directly to the head of the division. However, in the second division, the engineers were distributed among the three shops and, like the production workers, answered to various shop heads. Neither organizational structure is superior; they had just evolved in order to meet the circumstances within each division. Problems within the first division created a situation that required the engineers to learn from one another and to pool engineering resources. By contrast, issues that arose in the second division required the production and engineering people to cooperate at the level of the individual shops.[4]

Such organizational differences reflect the differing circumstances of the two divisions. As a result of these differences, the hierarchical structures evolved to take account of the issues. This sort of evolution is the very epitome of a people-centred living service – if the management had enforced a rigid organizational structure then the response to the problems which had arisen would not have been nearly so effective.

Three important ways to break organizational silos are: nurturing a co-operative mindset, collaborating across boundaries and leveraging organizational culture.

Nurture a cooperative mindset

In any global company, certain shared values and principles provide a foundation for the strategy, processes and people in each country in which a company does business. Alongside that, local subsidiaries are geared up to meet the challenges of local customers. An evolving living service is not one-size-fits-all but instead is moulded to suit the needs of the local market.

Many of the concepts that we have illustrated in this book started in Japan. The templates, which enable an acceleration of customer opportunities, are one such example. Instead of creating each service from scratch, this approach is all about identifying the common building blocks that can be used to build new services. Such templates represent the blocks that have been found to be the most usable and useful. Their design has been tried and tested. These blocks, in turn, can be used to build bigger and more complicated services.

This simple idea was initially concerned just with creating templates for infrastructure and products. It was not about *service*. As a result it was a solution driven to address the demands of the situation in Japan, not the global market.

An attribute of leadership is the ability to take a great idea from somewhere and be able to see its applicability elsewhere. In this regard, Lynda Gratton talks about fostering a cooperative mindset to enhance such opportunities. 'The emergence of a cooperative mindset', she writes, 'depends on leaders' attitudes towards cooperation and competition and their capacity and willingness to craft within the organization a sense of mutuality and collegiality.'[5] In other words, a key aspect of maximizing collective energy is in utilizing best practice and empowering people to adapt those ideas to make them even better.

In November 2003, David Courtley, the CEO of Fujitsu Services (the European arm of Fujitsu), visited Fujitsu's global headquarters in Tokyo. In a meeting room on the 32nd floor of Fujitsu's headquarters building in the city centre, he encountered this template approach for the first time.

When Courtley came across it, it was being used for providing infrastructure and products. It had been in operation for two years and more than 4,000 customers already had many solutions in Japan. He saw an opportunity. The approach was already reaping benefits in the Japanese market. It cut costs by making what we sold much simpler. It was delivered more quickly and was more reliable. And it was also more flexible while at the same time being more consistent.

Could this template approach be applied to services as well? Could it deliver cost-effective elegant simplicity and invisible excellence that customers wanted, and potentially revolutionize how we understand and deliver services?

Since 2003, ignited by David Courtley's initial enthusiasm, a group of people within Fujitsu have been turning the initial glimmer he identified into delivered practice that has helped transform Fujitsu's approach to service.

One of the people in the vanguard of the transformation is Alan Goswell. Goswell is a 'lifer' at the company. Goswell helped come up with a transformation plan for taking the template approach and turning it into a service-oriented solution with global implications. He realized that the traditional way IT companies worked was no longer sufficient. Traditionally, product companies have innovated their products, for example, continually releasing new versions of popular software programs. The customer then looked for a way of utilizing the product to turn it into something that would match their business needs. A service provider could, if needed, then run the product for them. The pace of change was very much driven by the product companies.

What Goswell learned is that customers do not actually want lots of change as this creates cost. What customers really want is stability. Taking this as his starting point, Goswell created a model by breaking down the existing one, which helped turn product-based thinking into a service deliverable. The result was the living service approach – where everything is based around satisfying the customer's business need.

This story shows how cooperation can take us all a long way. The spark of the idea in Japan, the foresight of Courtley and the adaptation made by Goswell all contributed to the creation and growth of living service. Ideas were brought together from various national and cultural contexts to produce something to the benefit of all. Across the field, energy flow was increased and energy was maximized – all due to a mindset of cooperation.

Prompt people to collaborate across boundaries

A collaborative mindset is at its most effective when it crosses boundaries. This is because, as Lynda Gratton explains, 'innovation ... arises when new ideas, from people in different groups and communities are brought together'. She goes on to say,

> A mindset of cooperation and the capacity for spanning boundaries creates a deep potential well ... of goodwill towards one another, they trust each other and they are prepared and able to work across boundaries.[6]

Just as no individual knows all the answers, no company or organization can work in isolation. We can all learn from each other – energy can be increased if we build from each other's respective knowledge and combine in new innovative ways. Collaborating across boundaries is a necessary tool to further our individual understanding and unleash the combined potential of all of us.

We have talked of the alliance between Microsoft and Fujitsu which has resulted in some innovative new technologies. The idea for a relationship between Microsoft and Fujitsu came from working together in the sales environment in 2003. Both Marilyn Slavin (then of Microsoft) and

Steve Walsh of Fujitsu saw the benefits of utilizing the best of each company. Microsoft is strong in software and at the time was coming up with a whole suite of new products such as Vista and Windows 2008 Server. Fujitsu, by contrast, is good at managing infrastructure and so appealed to Microsoft for its ability to integrate the software into an overall service proposition for customers. By working with Walsh, Slavin began to appreciate the benefits that the strong processes – such as the extensive pre-testing and integration of component modules – within Fujitsu could help benefit Microsoft in terms of cost reduction and producing a coherent product suite.

The first project run by both companies produced some startling results. Slavin recalled how after the project was completed she became convinced of the need to use the processes that Fujitsu had developed. Many practical benefits had emerged from following them – costs alone fell by more than 25 per cent. Moreover, the emphasis on pre-testing had helped build a business case for rationalizing the number of desktop alternatives for customers. Before, individuals within a company could have any flavour of Windows operating systems they wanted. Afterwards, they chose from a menu the combination which suited them best in their current environment. Such a change reduced not only the maintenance costs for the suppliers, but also the complexity and costs for the customer.

These technological benefits have to be seen, however, in the context of two very different companies working together. An innovative American software company and a process-oriented Japanese company make unlikely bedfellows. Walsh recalled how the values were very different between the companies. The values were divergent for a number of unrelated issues which meant overcoming them was an even greater challenge. For example, Fujitsu has expertise in services while Microsoft's focus is on its software products. Fujitsu's business is based around time whereas Microsoft's is around licences. It was even noted that Fujitsu was perceived to employ older staff compared to Microsoft! At all times, however, the people led by Slavin and Walsh were willing to learn from each other and share great ideas when they heard them.

Following the success of being awarded a number of contracts, the relationship began to develop. However, the difference in values continued to require attention and bridging. Walsh and Slavin realized the importance of empathy in developing their joint services. There was a basic need to be able to focus on what the person in the opposite company wanted. For example, Microsoft might want to know about the licensing implications for a deal whereas Fujitsu might not be so interested. Walsh discovered that these details were so much more important than basic rapport – to span boundaries properly people had to understand the sometimes alien values of a completely different company.

Slavin agreed that people needed to be diplomatic and rational to maximize the collective energy. People also needed always to think about the relationship going forward into the future. It was, in other words, of greater collective value than any one individual within it. Indeed, she mused, 'perhaps the relationship works because opposites attract – you respect something because you yourself don't have the skill set'. Certainly in living service, there is a recognition that in order to understand truly what the customer wants there needs to be an alignment of minds. For this, an adaptive, flexible skill-set is par for the course.

To illustrate this point, Walsh then concluded with an example. During one project there were lots of complaints about Microsoft from Fujitsu staff and about Fujitsu from Microsoft staff. The problems broadly stemmed from each side's understanding of how change within the delivery should be employed. Fujitsu was in charge of the change control process and understood a change in delivery would be costly and time-consuming for the customer. For Microsoft, however, change was desirable as it meant delivering the best technical solution possible for the customer. Both companies had the customer's best interests at heart, but there was tension between them. This issue was beginning to cause some bad blood between the two sides and even caused the customer to start raising a few concerns.

At this point, Slavin and Walsh got the teams together to understand each other's business case. The two sides simply had not appreciated the differing world-views which were causing the problems between themselves. After that meeting, the air was cleared and the relationship worked far better.

Spanning boundaries has been crucial to the success of Slavin and Walsh in managing the Fujitsu–Microsoft alliance. An empathetic understanding, together with an open mind, has contributed to a situation where the collective energy of both sides has been turned up to the maximum. And it is customers – such as Reuters – who are the key beneficiaries.

Prompting people to collaborate across organizational boundaries is not always an easy task. The Arthur Murray Dance Studio, an international chain of dance studios, claim that '… everyone has dance rhythms – we walk, speak, even work in rhythms'.[7] We think everyone has collaboration rhythms as well. All it needs is mind, body and soul in alignment for the rhythm of collaboration to come alive.

Leverage organizational culture

Every organization has a unique personality, its own DNA. What creates that personality is often hard to distil and understand both for outsiders looking in and insiders looking out. Understanding an organization's personality is important as it helps shape the way the people within the organization will work – and this is key to helping us maximize the collective energy.

A company's personality may be dependent on a number of factors. Its founders, its history, its business and its size are all important.

Fujitsu's people-focused and customer-oriented DNA can be traced back to the company's first president at its founding in 1935 as a manufacturer of telephone equipment. He exhorted that people should, 'never become complacent, no matter how experienced you become'. He added, 'always think from a customer-centric perspective', and, at all times, 'have a passion for research and exploration'.

Later, president Okada, the leader who established the present direction of Fujitsu, delivered his message to 'aspire to unlimited growth'. He continued, 'Let us move ahead with courage'. President Okada also launched the High Reliability Initiative in 1966. In his view, many factors determine a product's superiority – such as cost, function and quality. Of these, he put quality above everything else. Later Fujitsu's approach to quality was further extended by Hiromasa Kimura, our Special Advisor in Quality Management, who stated 'Dignity inspires everyone across the organization to contribute to superior quality in all activities undertaken for customers.'

Another Fujitsu leader, Toshio Ikeda, discussed earlier in this chapter, led the company into the computer business. His contributions at Fujitsu are known as the Doctrines of Toshio Ikeda. One interesting doctrine is,

'When you can't make up your mind over a difficult choice, trust your people. If a decision turns out to be wrong, correct it immediately.'

In 1984, the company's former president Kobayashi left a slogan for everyone across Fujitsu, 'Just give it a try' – where he urged all to rely on their own experience in doing their work. Two years later, the next president, Yamamoto established 'What mankind can dream, technology can achieve' as the company motto. Later this was rephrased as 'Turning dreams into reality'.

In 1998, Naoyuki Akikusa became president. With his deep experience, Akikusa contributed greatly in transforming Fujitsu – particularly with regard to an expansion of the services business. Realizing the potential of the internet early on, he introduced his concept, 'everything on the internet' in 1999. This was at a time before many businesses had appreciated the potential of the internet. Under his leadership, Fujitsu documented 'The FUJITSU Way' in January 2002. This had the objective of getting every employee to clearly understand the company's basic management ethos, its mission, sense of values and code of conduct.

'The FUJITSU Way' is the core set of principles under which the Fujitsu Group 'strives for continuous development as a global corporation and to help achieve a sustainable society'. It guides the corporate and individual action of the Fujitsu Group and our commitment to sustainability. It provides a common understanding of Fujitsu's mission, values and code of conduct. It also serves as the standard for governing individual employees' business activities, as well as the driving force behind the company's socially responsible business activities. To allow people continuously to create knowledge and contribute to the performance of the company, Akikusa also established Fujitsu University which delivers a number of courses including an executive training programme known as the Global Knowledge Institute (GKI). These courses are in line with The FUJITSU Way. Akikusa is now Chairman of the Fujitsu Group.

Under our current president Hiroaki Kurokawa, there was an initial focus on a transformation of business processes to enable a change in mindset and behaviour of each and every employee. Everyone throughout the company was expected to share a sense of urgency, focus on the realities of the front lines of business, ensure open communications and discuss negative issues. Kurokawa also re-emphasized the importance of thinking and acting from the customers' perspective, maintaining quality, on-time delivery and accelerating the speed of actions. As Fujitsu is both an IT service provider and a product manufacturer, Kurokawa is driving operational excellence in both 'factory' and the 'field.' In Ted Levitt's words, manufacturing occurs in the factory, while service is provided out there in the field. Kurokawa is now also emphasizing 'field innovation' to 'bring innovation to companies, people's lives and society at large'.

Continuously strive in the wider business ecosystem

While it is too much of a generalization to say that Western cultures inherently favour individualism and Eastern cultures inherently favour the group, there is some truth in the assertion. An individual, particularly a junior member of a team, will react and contribute in different ways in a meeting depending on the nation that they are in. While forcefully countering a point may be seen as a manifestation of strong independent thinking in the UK or USA, it may be seen as highly childish and immature in Japan. Within this context, the way people respond to the strategic direction and processes within differing cultures is likely to produce different results. This means, as we have already discussed, that living service varies between nations.

And the great point here is that this does not matter. Living service will evolve differently depending on the nation in which it is delivered – but this will be because the people within the supplier and customer in that nation may interact in a different way from other people in another country. So long as both supplier and customer are happy with the result, the exact form of the living service is allowed to adapt to the appropriate shape. Living service is a synthesis of Mind-Body-Soul after all, and, like the Mind-Body-Soul of any other living entity, it will produce unique but always positive results.

One story illustrates this point. Rodney Hobbs works for Fujitsu in Australia. In 2004, a request came from Fujitsu in Japan for an Australian representative to attend a workshop on a new way of modularizing products to benefit customers. Following a discussion with his manager, Hobbs was sent to investigate further. The workshop consisted of 40 people gathered from the furthest reaches of the company, all brought together to learn this new way of delivering added value to customers. The workshop covered how Fujitsu in Japan was re-organizing itself to meet customers' needs more closely, reduce costs and improve reliability by taking a template approach. However, like Goswell, Hobbs understood the market that Fujitsu Australia operated in had a much greater focus on services than products, and that the new process would need to be adapted to work. He met a number of like-minded people who were also more focused on services who immediately began to work with him on adapting the approach. And just as immediately they started to run into problems.

The Australian operations, like Fujitsu's operations in many other parts of the globe, provided traditional end-to-end IT services. This means they could do everything from the very large, for example design, build and run a customer's business system, to the very small, like providing a customer with a single PC. This business had largely grown in a fragmented fashion. As a result, Fujitsu had lots of customers, doing lots of different things. There was, in other words, little commonality across the business.

Following the workshop in Japan, Hobbs believed that there must be a better way to operate, a way that could bring standardization to the offered services, so that investments could be targeted to supply the greatest benefit to the greatest number of customers.

An early problem he faced was that the business didn't recognize a need to change as the benefits of the new way were not clear to all. Existing customers were happy and new business was being won – so why fix what was not broken? Hobbs recognized that this was a very internal view – he believed that customers were happy because they didn't understand what was actually possible – what Fujitsu actually could deliver. He was sure that customer's expectations could be exceeded if a new approach was used, an approach built on understanding commonalities between what different customers wanted and then standardizing services to them.

The CEO of Fujitsu in Australia, Rod Vawdrey, saw that there was value in this fledgling idea and provided Hobbs the commitment and leadership to work on business plans to prove it could actually deliver value to the business. Vawdrey said at the time, 'My greatest challenge was to understand where and how to apply the new way, while still shaping the business within the current model. Finding the balance was the key and the results have supported our growth and success.' All of this meant that to most people in Fujitsu Australia Hobbs was, as he himself describes, 'a guy who no-one knows what he does, with a role no-one's written down, doing this thing no-one understands, in a company that was not leveraging its foundation for sustainable growth in a very competitive and mature market'.

However, the people Hobbs had met from around the world at the workshop in Japan also felt that they could create a service transformation and they had begun to build support in their own countries. Soon a worldwide virtual team began to emerge including people like Goswell. Their shared vision created what Hobbs describes as, 'a family. It doesn't matter where you are or when you last spoke, when you connect it was like yesterday'. As the people began to develop ideas, a clearer picture began to emerge of what this transformation would look like. Eventually the simple Four Row Model began to take shape and, more importantly, customers began to understand what it meant to them. Hobbs told us: 'The great thing is, it's a simple model, it's common sense; that's the beauty of it, its simplicity.' He goes on, 'and it's not something we do only to our customers, it's something we do to ourselves'.

Through the persistence to overcome any challenge and with the support of his colleagues and CEO, Hobbs energetically helped to drive service change across Fujitsu in Australia. Why was he so passionate? His answer is simple and telling: 'I had the opportunity to be part of changing the company. How many people get that shot?'

The importance of people within an organization and the wider business ecosystem has never been greater. Champions of change like Dorgan, Simpson, Goswell, Slavin, Walsh and Hobbs have far-reaching influence. By working with people across the boundaries of the organization, customers, partners and the wider business ecosystem, they have all driven transformation in order to continually provide great service. While products can be produced anywhere and at any time, service – great service – needs strong people-focused interaction in order to give it shape and direction. Processes and strategies must be shaped by people to give the customer the service they demand and deserve. Just as concepts such as total quality management and lean production became the clarion calls of industry in the past, so a people-oriented living service which can adapt and evolve to the demands of the customer will be the call of the future.

In summary

Champions of change contribute to developing living service by inspiring a people-focused service culture; changing the game by doing things differently; continually engaging with customers; accelerating customers' opportunities; orchestrating the delivery of great service to customers; co-creating the future with a long-term view; and maximizing the collective energy of people via their championing activities.

To find champions of change in your organizations, we suggest you look for the following attributes in people's characteristics. All champions demonstrate at least one and often many of these attributes:

◆ *Hungry*: Champions of change are conscious and eager to continually *learn–break–create* to realize their vision. In Japanese this cycle is known as *shu-ha-ri*. This means that continual learning and relearning is required in order always to challenge the status quo. This arises out of *biishiki* – aesthetic values or personal sense of beauty – and people's past experiences. The foresight and synthesizing capabilities of champions contribute to stimulate innovation.

◆ *Hot*: They are passionate about and are confident in their convictions. Champions of change aim for results by developing new ideas and creating knowledge – by both tacit and explicit means – with a great sense of timing. Sometimes this will drive them to break organizational norms. Their *zenshin-zenrei* – wholehearted commitment – helps them to *learn–break–create* continually.

◆ *Harmonious*: Champions of change think holistically. They maintain a rhythm for balanced relationships with all people inside and outside their organizations. They create and sustain 'hot spots' in their organizations.[8]

◆ *Humble*: Although they are passionate about their ideas they are not constrained by them. They always listen carefully to others, learn from them, and then use their own intuition. They share great ideas when they hear them.

◆ *Healthy*: Champions of change are energetic enough to persistently overcome any challenges they face. They are resilient enough to transform their challenges into irresistible energy for continuous innovations.

Agenda 7 – Maximize Collective Energy

◆ Ensure people can realize their own and their customers' dreams

◆ Break organizational silos

◆ Continuously strive to thrive in the wider business ecosystem.

These are not mere bullet points; they are the means of maximizing the energy of people for continuing the rhythms that help deliver living service.

Epilogue:
Sustaining Service

S ervice can only be successful in the longer term if it continually adapts and evolves to the changing needs of customers and their customers. In order to do this, service providers must understand, honour and respond to the Mind-Body-Soul of customers throughout the service journey. Their approach needs to combine art – the people who are in tune with customers, accelerating their opportunities, and delivering great service – and science – utilizing proven methodologies and enabling technologies. Such art and science can only be sustained by people.

We have been fortunate enough to work with many organizations – customers, partners, suppliers – which have brought all these things together to contribute genuinely to our continuing journey towards living service excellence.

The world today

In the world today, there is an ongoing debate on the optimal balance between ownership and access for any particular service. An example of this is libraries. Traditionally, libraries were viewed as 'warehouses of information'. But, with the rapid advancement of technology and the way people want to have access to information, libraries are being reinvented as 'providers of access to information'. Laura T. Kane, a catalogue librarian at the School of Medicine, University of South Carolina, emphasizes 'humankind will never quench its thirst for knowledge' and the choices will not be either access or ownership, rather a combination of the best features of both the traditional warehouse idea (ownership) and the electronic library idea (access) for library services.[1] This idea of combining traditional and modern thinking could be also applicable to any other services.

In the area of IT, many organizations are looking to find their optimal balance between accessing information services and owning IT systems. A great IT service provider can help its customers by allowing them to find the balance that is most appropriate for them. This can be done by making processes and benefits transparent, and then communicating these in the language of the customer. After all, great service is always about fitting the right service to the customer; not trying to fit the customer to the service.

In a different sphere, as we were writing this book we came across a service promotion video entitled '6 star service' produced by a collection of major luxury marques. The companies included Maybach cars, Bookajet (an executive charter jet company) and Greycoat Placements (suppliers of domestic staff to private households). The service they spoke of goes beyond 5 star and really takes service to a whole new level. The key elements are that the service must be personalized or tailored; it needs to provide things that the customer does not anticipate; it needs to be seamless and invisible so that the customer does not even notice it; and, finally, in order to deliver great service, businesses must always listen to their customers.

In a similar vein, one of the finest hotels in Japan, the Conrad Tokyo, talks of a service philosophy they call 'Silent Symphony.' This is designed to deliver pleasurable, graceful, calm and unobtrusive service to their guests. Like an orchestra, it values the skills of the individual hotel staff member while realizing the need of the team to function seamlessly and consistently. The result is that they appreciate how every interaction with a guest directly reflects on their reputation and how their team members should be treated with the same respect as their guests.

All these attributes sound great, don't they? But how many people can afford to enjoy such '6 star services' or stay at the Conrad Tokyo?

In our continuing journey towards living service, we are now trying to make the appropriate balance between access and ownership while also making our services accessible, affordable, enjoyable and sustainable through a combination of standardization and customization to meet customers' needs. This will allow more people to enjoy elegant simplicity and invisible excellence with less cost and pain. To deliver living service, we relentlessly pursue continuous innovation in all of our activities, ranging from our engagement with customers to co-creating the future with our customers, partners and suppliers.

We hope this book has demonstrated the importance of the holistic view – Mind-Body-Soul – in delivering service excellence in the business world. Yet any message which hopes to have lasting influence cannot just be concerned with the insular, perhaps parochial, needs of today's business alone.

Imagine a day in the future when organizations will select their service providers by considering not only the economic benefits, but also social and environmental imperatives. That day is already here. Environmental awareness is now a fact of life. Research consistently suggests that over half of consumers are more likely to purchase from green companies, and the vast majority prefer to work for green companies. So going green makes a company attractive to both customers and potential employees.

Are you ready?

Beyond today

Already in Europe there is a flood of new directives covering hazardous waste, landfill, packaging, battery disposal and so on. The onus is now on businesses: 'producer responsibility' is the new mantra.

Getting it wrong can have ruinous effects on a company's reputation and performance. Global communications mean that disgust at a company for an environmental or social breach can quickly turn into a global boycott. While environmental issues are certainly in the news today, a wider corporate social responsibility agenda is emerging very quickly. Increasingly, companies are collaborating to address social, economic and environmental concerns as they do business.

You can either see all this as an extra burden or a glorious opportunity. We prefer the latter view. The new legislative and highly monitored environment gives businesses the opportunity to gain greater control within their own supply chains and also learn more about their suppliers. The result of this additional information could be an opportunity to cut costs and enhance the reputation of the company. Within this context, the many components of living service can help provide pointers which can add additional value to a company seeking to demonstrate a responsible attitude.

First, the focus on a long-term view that living service encourages has positive sustainability benefits.

Secondly, the use of templates for service design and management allows you to deliver elegant simplicity. The benefits can be seen in terms of reduced complexity, dynamic reporting and live analysis of economic, social and environmental performance.

Thirdly, the use of a service management framework based on pre-tested and pre-verified templates allows for prompt compliance with changing standards as these are developed, for example, by substituting improved components within the service as they become available.

Fourthly, the focus on continuous innovation can lead to sustainable services. Within the people-centred environment, if one of the customer's business goals is influenced by sustainability concerns, living service can adapt and evolve to meet such concerns.

Let us look at each of these areas in more detail.

Long-term sustainability

Long-term thinking is a key element of living service. The use of best practice templates and pre-testing together with a long-term view can all contribute towards a sustainable future.

Since 1997, for example, the Toyota Prius has been one of the world's leading hybrid electric vehicles. It has one of the best fuel economies and lowest carbon dioxide emissions among all cars. Yet in an interview with *Business Week*, Toyota CEO Katsuaki Watanabe said that Toyota was 'aiming at reducing, by half, both size and cost of the third-generation hybrid system'.[2] In other words, the car will go through continuous development to provide further sustainable improvements in its fuel efficiencies. Indeed, the word *prius* is the Latin word meaning 'to go before', and Toyota chose this name as they saw the Prius vehicle as the forerunner of cars to come.

Since its establishment in 1935, Fujitsu has made environmental conservation one of the most important elements in the company's management and one of the core values in 'The FUJITSU Way'. Environmental initiatives are promoted at grass-roots level as part of the company's environmental action programmes. There are five priority areas: improving the environmental value of products and services; global warming countermeasures (reducing harmful emissions from factories and offices); reinforcing governance (improving our environmental manage-ment system); risk management (advancing green procurement activities); and environmental contributions to society.

We anticipate that in the future people will expect services that will allow them to access information that is personalized and delivered when they need them. To respond to such emerging needs, we are continually innovating to realize our long-term vision, which we call 'Information@Hand'. This will enable people to become an integral part of the field where they work (recall Levitt, where service is provided out there in the field) and environ-ment where they live and thrive. In our efforts towards realizing Information@Hand, we are combining both tacit and explicit dimensions of knowledge to make it a people-oriented, sustainable service of the future.

The use of templates for service development and delivery allows the delivery of elegant simplicity against complexity. Such an approach can further boost sustainability. Reporting and performance modules can be geared to provide reporting and management information on areas of ser-vice which provide an environmental or social impact. Not only that, but they can help get to the root cause of why the impact is being caused. A property company with a large building portfolio, for example, could have each building monitored for their respective carbon dioxide footprints. The buildings with the largest footprints could then be considered in the light of understanding what it is about the better performing buildings that makes them preferable. In this way, the reporting module can enforce best practice and continuous innovation for the company concerned. An example of this is Fujitsu's own buildings in the UK. Some 1,514 tonnes of CO_2 were saved in 2006–2007 and £750,000 of costs were saved on our annual electricity bill. This was achieved by implementing half-hourly electricity monitoring with rigorous reporting across major UK sites, and then making sure we were using the building management systems prop-erly – for example, not keeping air conditioning running at weekends or during holidays or late at night, and reducing lighting and air conditioning in empty buildings.

The use of templates can also enforce best practice in sustainability. Consider an IT service which provides doctors in a hospital with a portable device that gives real-time medicine prescription information. By redesigning the device so that it uses a lithium battery, the service can continue but with a lower environmental impact. Not only is the lithium battery, easier to recycle and dispose of, but it can also be recharged and reused. By splitting services into constituent parts, the 'polluting' elements, such as the battery, can be worked on and improved. When the new battery is ready, extensive testing takes place before it becomes part of the new template and so part of the service. This upgrade takes place while the service is continuing to provide the customer with what they need. The service thus evolves in a sustainable manner.

The next area to consider is continuous innovation. In Fujitsu, there have been a number of areas of recent innovation within the environmental sphere. New bio-based plastics, for example, made from corn and other plant starches have been developed, which require less oil to produce. Such plastics can be used in fabricating laptop PC housings. Another example is a photocatalyst that dissolves dirt and stains using ultraviolet rays. This means that chemical forms of stain removal which have a high environmental impact can be scaled back.

We believe the overall approach of living service can aid sustainability. This is because living service is people-centred and people are very good at sharing their needs and concerns. If a customer's customer were to raise certain environmental concerns, for example, those concerns would be transferred to the customer. For instance, demand for organic food leads a supermarket to respond by making more available on its shelves. Such a customer requires a service provider who can make a similar response. So the supermarket will then challenge its farming suppliers to provide a greater proportion of organic crops.

With the benefit of a long-term view, templates and continued innovation, service providers can act sustainably more easily and cost-efficiently. But it is the people themselves within the customer and supplier who will really make the difference. People are the Soul of the organization who can champion change and adapt the processes that make sure such concerns are properly addressed.

Interconnected whole

We live on a small, crowded and fragile planet. All of us are part of an interconnected whole. Business must play its part in addressing the social, economic and environmental concerns that are growing with an ever louder voice year on year.

'Protection of the earth's environment is now a pressing worldwide issue', Fujitsu chairman Naoyuki Akikusa emphasized, going on to say:

> *Environmental protection is no longer merely an issue impacting the sustainability of individual corporations, but is now critical to the continued existence of economic society itself. We believe that adequately protecting the earth's environment requires not only improvements that extend earlier efforts, but major innovations as well.* [3]

Moreover, we think that the role of IT in protecting the global environment will become even larger. We must reduce the environmental burden associated with the use of IT. As the use of IT expands, reducing power consumption and increasing recycling are, of course, required, but reducing the environmental burden associated with the manufacture of IT equipment is also a major theme.

An example of business already working in this way can be seen in the relationship Fujitsu now has with Reuters. Within our contract, a framework for corporate responsibility in community, social and environmental affairs was agreed. In this context, the solution was designed to address these affairs. Double-sided printers will be deployed, for instance, to reduce paper use. The whole computing infrastructure has been designed to minimize carbon emissions through using less power-hungry terminals.

In the same context, in August 2007, Fujitsu announced a £44 million investment in a new high specification green data centre. The new data centre will be used by companies and public bodies in the UK and continental Europe. The 65,000 square-foot data centre will be designed with the latest environmental features which, together with an IT modernization programme, will save enough electricity to power up to 6,000 homes every year, equivalent to saving an annual 10,000 tonnes of carbon dioxide.

By redeveloping a brownfield site and refurbishing an existing warehouse, Fujitsu will reduce the overall environmental impact. The intelligent cooling system in conjunction with variable speed fans, pumps and heat exchangers significantly reduces the energy used to keep the IT systems cool. Additionally, Fujitsu will reduce the power consumption of the customer IT systems housed in the data centre through a modernization programme. Consolidating the IT systems within the data centre will achieve power consumption and cost savings of up to 50 per cent, compared to current usage.

Martin Provoost, Fujitsu's head of data centres in Europe, says:

Companies have realized that expanding their data centres to cope with IT growth is expensive and wastes resources. They need lower costs and want their data centres and systems to be efficient and planet friendly.

In the longer term, service has to adapt and evolve not just to meet changing customer needs, but also the wider changing needs of our planet. It is our belief that the proper understanding and application of the principles of living service can not only allow service providers of every kind to deliver great service, but will also help to promote a sustainable future. But someone has to lead – to thrive collaboratively in this fragile planet, someone has to issue a call to action.

Call to action

Living service does not exist in a vacuum. In our minds, there is no doubt that organizations now need to transform themselves to thrive sustainably in a changing world. Sustainability is more than just a fashion; it is an essential strategy. Only companies that embrace it will themselves be sustainable in the long run. All of us in business must learn to consider economic, social and environmental imperatives, in order to thrive in the hypercompetitive global market, with increasing pressure from environmental lawmakers, and more importantly conscious customers who care more about the health and happiness of future generations.

Through the use of the methods indicated above, and the overall approach of living service, a multidisciplinary, people-centred collaborative effort can be promoted. Achieving this will require a level of collaboration across different organizations on a scale not seen before. The lifeblood of knowledge that flows within organizations, between their sales, development, delivery and innovation functions, will need to be extended out to customers, partners and suppliers, and beyond to customers' customers.

In his article, 'A better way to innovate', the limitations of a siloed mentality were made clearer by Henry W. Chesbrough. 'Information now flows cheaply and instantaneously over the internet; smart people are more widely dispersed but more closely connected than ever before. Ideas bubble up in organizations of all kinds and sizes, not just in large research labs.'[4] Dorothy Leonard-Barton also showed how to build and sustain the sources of innovation in her book *Wellsprings of Knowledge*. She argued how the responsibility stays with people, 'for selecting the correct knowledge sources, for understanding how knowledge is accessed and channelled, and for redirecting flows'.[5]

We propose a model where communication, knowledge sharing and collaboration can occur among currently siloed organizations. Such a multi-disciplinary collaboration model needs to span across industries, universities, NGOs (non-governmental organizations), NPOs (non-profit organizations), governments and individuals (see Figure 8.1).

FIGURE 8.1 ◆ **Multidisciplinary Collaboration Model**

In our view, a 'consciousness community' (shown in Figure 8.1), consisting of individuals with insightful messages, is emerging. In his documentary film series, 'Gaia Symphony,' Jin Tatsumura shows how, 'individuals with very insightful messages are making an extraordinary contribution to help create a beautiful future for the planet earth'.[6] By connecting all the dots, fostering collaboration and using the wellsprings of knowledge around the globe – explicit and tacit – in this way, the promise of a sustainable future can be fulfilled.

Many people are already championing sustainability. They range from inventors to activists, tycoons to politicians. For example, they include the Gaia theorist James Lovelock, who theorized that the earth is a living system. 'Gaia works only because it is open to the universe, powered not by finite internal stores of fuel but by the endless flow of solar energy through the system as a whole', notes Lovelock.[7]

The former US vice-president Al Gore has also sparked a global movement with his award-winning documentary film, '*An Inconvenient Truth*' and also won a Nobel Peace prize. Together with the UN's Intergovernmental Panel for Climate Change, he is helping to contribute to understanding the measures required to combat global warming.[8] These are only two examples of many thousands of people who are becoming more and more conscious about the future of our planet, which itself is a living system, continuously adapting and evolving its ecosystem.

We have all heard of the 'butterfly effect' – the idea, for example, that a single butterfly flapping its wings in Tokyo could cause a hurricane (or prevent it happening) in New York.[9] We strongly believe it is possible for people as well as organizations to make a huge difference – even change the world – with the slightest efforts at just the right time and in just the right place.

One might ask why we should bother making a difference for others on our planet. Business books generally do not try to emphasize social, economic and environmental sustainability. We believe that business can help provide models and ways of working which can help contribute towards addressing the wider concerns we are all facing. The concepts which cover the Mind, Body and Soul which we have introduced in this book – such as being people-focused; being enabled by people and optimized by processes and technology; transparency; delivering invisible excellence and elegant simplicity through continuous innovation; and finally adaptability – are all traits which can contribute to the ongoing sustainability debate.

At a wider level, an organic, evolving living service can also be seen as a metaphor for the way we as individuals can work together to overcome our common challenges. We invite individuals as well as organizations of any discipline, any culture, and any geography to join us in co-creating a sustainable future, utilizing the principles of living service. The future belongs to us all.

Appendix:
Your Living Service Agenda

Agenda 1 – Develop a Living Service Culture

- Everything you do, do around customers and their customers
- Earn the trust of your customers and employees
- Put people at the centre of everything
- Empower champions of change
- Nurture your supply chain
- Take the long-term view

Agenda 2 – Change the Game

- Make customers' needs transparent
- Grow together with customers and their customers
- Consider people as your key differentiator
- Leverage tacit knowledge
- Focus on invisible excellence and elegant simplicity

Agenda 3 – Engage with Customers

- Focus on understanding the customer's journey
- Help customers with their decision-making
- Continually engage with customers
- Take a consistent approach to the customer throughout the journey

Agenda 4 – Accelerate Customers' Opportunities

- Focus on elegant simplicity
- Make processes transparent
- Turn problems into opportunities

Agenda 5 – Deliver Great Service

- Strive to deliver invisible excellence
- Ensure delivery is in tune with the customer
- Make delivery scalable

Agenda 6 – Co-create the Future

- Continually collaborate with the customer
- Enable all to contribute to the customer's journey
- Co-evolve with your partners and suppliers

Agenda 7 – Maximize Collective Energy

- Ensure people can realize their own and their customers' dreams
- Break organizational silos
- Continuously strive to thrive in the wider business ecosystem.

Notes

Introduction: Inside Living Service

1 James P. Womack, Daniel T. Jones and Daniel Roos, *The Machine that Changed the World*, Free Press, New York, 1990

2 Katsuaki Watanabe, interviewed by Thomas A. Stewart and Anand P. Raman, 'Lessons from Toyota's Long Drive', *Harvard Business Review*, July–August 2007, pp. 74–83

3 Dan Jones attributed these words around the launch of the book he co-authored: James P. Womack and Daniel T. Jones, *Lean Solutions*, Simon & Schuster, New York, 2005.

4 *Toyota in the World 2007*, Toyota Motor Corporation, Tokyo, May 2007, p. 2

5 Stuart Crainer, 'The Next Internet Revolution', *The Times*, London, 15 June 2002.

6 Ted Levitt, 'Production-Line Approach to Service' in *Ted Levitt on Marketing*, Harvard Business School Press, Boston, 2006, p. 59

7 Georg Krogh, Kazuo Ichijo, Ikujiro Nonaka, *Enabling Knowledge Creation*, Oxford University Press, New York, 2000, p. 197.

Chapter 1: Developing a Living Service Culture

1 Ted Levitt, 'Marketing Myopia', *Harvard Business Review*, July–August 2004, pp. 138–49

2 Stuart Crainer, 'The Next Internet Revolution, *The Times*, London, 15 June 2002.

3 Source data around price margins is 'Dairy Supply Chain Margins, 2005–6', Milk Development Council, October 2006, pp. 4–5. To summarize, in 1995 the average price of a pint of milk in the UK was 42.1p, of which the dairy farmer would get 24.5p and the retailer 1.3p. In 2005, the price was 50.9p, the farmer getting 18.5p and the retailer getting 15.6p. Supermarket response and National Farmers' Union quotation: press release from Tesco PLC on 3 April 2007 – 'Tesco announces direct deal for UK dairy farmers'. To summarize, Tesco raised its offer price to farmers to 22 per litre.

Chapter 2: Changing the Game

1 Tom Brown, Stuart Crainer and Des Dearlove, *Business Minds*, Financial Times Prentice Hall, London, 2003, p. 126

2 W. Chan Kim and Renée Mauborgne, 'Value Innovation: The Strategic Logic of High Growth', *Harvard Business Review*, July 2004, pp. 172–80

3 Ikujiro Nonaka, 'The Knowledge-Creating Company', *Harvard Business Review*, July–August 2007, p. 165

4 Ikujiro Nonaka *et al.*, 'The Power of Tacit Knowledge', *Knowledge Management*, July/August 2001, pp. 10–15

Chapter 5: Delivering Great Service

1 Malcolm Gladwell, *Blink*, Penguin Books, London, 2007, pp. 133–36

Chapter 6: Co-creating The Future

1 C.K. Prahalad and G. Hamel, *Competing for the Future*, Harvard Business School Press, Boston, 1994

2 C.K. Prahalad and Venkat Ramaswamy, *The Future of Competition Co-Creating Unique Value with Customers*, Harvard Business School Press, Boston, 2003

Chapter 7: Maximizing Collective Energy

1 Mary Shelley, *Frankenstein* (1818), this edition 2003, Penguin, London, p. 58

2 Lynda Gratton, *Living Strategy*, Financial Times Prentice Hall, London, 2000

3 Lynda Gratton, *Hot Spots*, Berrett-Koehler Publishers, Inc., San Francisco, 2007, p. 3 and p. 13

4 Steven Spear and H. Kent Bowen, 'Decoding the DNA of the Toyota Production System', *Harvard Business Review*, September 1999, pp. 96–106.

5 Lynda Gratton, *Hot Spots*, Berrett-Koehler Publishers, Inc., San Francisco, 2007, p. 3

6 Lynda Gratton, *Hot Spots*, Berrett-Koehler Publishers, Inc., San Francisco, 2007, p. 3

7 Richard Smith and Mohi Ahmed, *Dance with your Collaborators*, Research Technology Management, September–October 2000, 43, 5, pp. 58–60

8 Lynda Gratton, *Hot Spots*, Berrett-Koehler Publishers, Inc., San Francisco, 2007

Epilogue: Sustaining Service

1 Laura Townsend Kane, 'Access vs. Ownership: Do we have to make a choice? *Interlending & Document Supply*, 28, 3, 2000, pp. 116–22

2 Ian Rowley, 'Toyota's Bid for a Better Battery', *Business Week*, 5 March 2007, *The Corporation*, online extra – http://www.businessweek.com/magazine/content/07_10/b4024075.htm

3 Naoyuki Akikusa, quote taken from *Fujitsu Group Sustainability Report 2007*, Fujitsu Limited, Tokyo, 2007, p. 3

4 Henry W. Chesbrough, 'A better way to innovate', *Harvard Business Review*, July 2003, pp. 12–13

5 Dorothy Leonard-Barton, *Wellsprings of Knowledge*, Harvard Business School Press, Boston, 1995, p. xiii

6 Jin Tatsumura's *Gaia Symphony* was first released in 1992 and consists of six documentary films detailing the messages of various extraordinary individuals. Further information can be found at http://gaiasymphony.com/

7 Oliver Morton, *Time*, Asia Edition, Hong Kong, 29 October 2007, p. 48

8 Carl Pope, *Time*, Asia Edition, Hong Kong, 29 October 2007, p. 42

9 Edward N. Lorenz (Professor Emeritus of Massachusetts Institute of Technology) is known for the 'Butterfly Effect'.

Index

access vs ownership 18, 20, 140–1
Accor 52–3
adaptation 14–15, 16, 26
affinity schemes 15
aircraft 1
airlines 10, 97–100, 115
  Virgin Atlantic 12–13
Akikusa, Naoyuki 134, 146
Allianz 40–1, 53, 74–5, 103
anticipation of change 109–10
Arthur Murray Dance Studio 133
ASIC (Allianz Shared Infrastructure
    Services) 40–1, 53
ATMs 51, 93–4
Australia 37, 135–7
automated telephone systems 8–9
automation 41, 78–9
  see also technology

B-pad 108
bakery analogy 65–70, 85, 87, 102
Ballmer, Steve 76
banking 1, 47–8, 51–2
  "la Caixa" 92–4
batteries 144–5
Bazalgette, Joseph 16–17
Beefeater pub/restaurant chain 59, 60
bio-based plastics 145
body, mind and soul 5, 22–5, 30, 64,
    118
Bookajet 141
boundaries, collaboration across
    130–3

Bourke, Paul 37
breakfast briefings 111–12
Brewer's Fayre pub/restaurant chain
    59, 60
BT 76
business ecosystem 135–7
butterfly effect 149

CA 75, 76
cabin crew 12–13
Caixa d'Estalvis i Pensions de
    Barcelona ("la Caixa") 92–4
call centres 9–10
carbon dioxide footprints 144
cars 1–3, 20–1, 82, 113, 143
celebrations 38
champions of change 43–4, 137, 138
  allowing them to lead 124–5
  attributes 138
  sustainability 149
change 23, 50–61
  anticipating change that will affect
    customers 109–10
  assisting customers with 110
  champions of *see* champions of
    change
  focus on invisible excellence and
    elegant simplicity 59–61
  growing together with customers and
    their customers 53–6
  leveraging tacit knowledge 57–9
  people as key differentiator 56–7
  transparency of customers' needs 53

Chesbrough, Henry W. 147–8
choice 18–20, 50–1
cholera epidemic 16–17
'CIO connect' events 111–12
Cisco 45, 75
co-evolving with partners and suppliers 113–15
collaboration
  across boundaries 130–3
  continuous collaboration with the customer 82–3, 106–12
  with partners and suppliers 113–15
  and sustainability 147–9
collective energy 25, 119–39
  breaking organizational silos 127–35
  change champions' attributes 138
  ensuring people can realize their own and their customers' dreams 122–7
  people at centre of corporate strategy 121–2
  striving in wider business ecosystem 135–7
commitment 121, 138
communication 1, 91
  straight talking 76–8
  unified communications 45–6
computing revolution 123–4
Conrad Tokyo hotel 141
consciousness community 148, 149
consistency 83–4, 89–90
continuous innovation see innovation
cooperative mindset 128–30
Corolla car 113
corporate responsibility 142, 146
corporate strategy 120–2
Costa Coffee 59
courier company 7
Courtley, David 129, 130
Cram, Tony 39–40
credit cards 14–15
crocodile 55
cross-functional approach 112–13

culture 23, 31–49
  earning trust of customers and employees 37–9
  empowering employees 43–4
  focus on customers and their customers 33–7
  long-termism 46–8
  national 135–7
  nurturing supply chain 44–6
  organizational 133–5
  people at the centre 39–42
customer engagement 25, 72, 73–84
  consistent approach to customer 83–4
  continual 82–3
  focus on understanding customer's journey 73–81
  helping customers with their decision-making 81–2
  and living service culture 33–7
Customer Experience Centres 111
customer satisfaction 4–5, 31–2
  measuring 48
customer surveys 82–3
customers
  allowing them to focus on their customers 78–9
  continual collaboration with 82–3, 106–12
  culture centred around customers and their customers 33–7
  designing services around 56
  earning trust of 37–9
  growing together with 53–6
  helping with their decision-making 81–2
  monitoring movements of 108
customer's journey
  enabling all to contribute to 112–13
  understanding 73–81
customer's needs 25, 67
  challenging existing assumptions and delivering extra value 76–8

customer's needs (*continued*)
  making them transparent 53, 68
  ensuring delivery is in tune with tacit
    needs 100–2
  and sustainability 145
  walking in customer's shoes to
    understand tacit needs 79–81

dairy suppliers 45, 153
data centre 146–7
data storage space 109–10
decision-making 81–2
delivery 96–104
  Four Row Model 25, 65–70, 70–2
  in tune with the customer 100–2
  scalability 102–4
  striving to deliver invisible excellence
    96–100
Dell 75, 76, 125
Dell, Michael 76
differentiation 52
  people as key differentiator 56–7
DMR 54–5
Dorgan, Mark 125–7, 137
dreams, realization of 122–7
Dregis 40
Drucker, Peter 48

electricity 15–16
  monitoring 144
elegant simplicity 12–14, 16, 26
  focus on 59–61, 85–90
emotion 42–3
employees 42
  earning trust of 37–9
  empowering 10, 43–4
energy 121
  collective *see* collective energy
energy company 77–8
engaging with customers *see* customer
  engagement
environmental protection 142, 145–6
  see also sustainability

Esmond, Don 113
European help desk 100–1
evolution 14–15, 16, 26
  co-evolving with partners and
    suppliers 113–15
extended warranty companies 51

FACOM 100 123
failure, impossibility of 38–9
field vs factory 4
film industry 32
finance departments 36
financial services 35–6
  see also banking
FLAG day (Feel Like A Guest day) 80
flexibility 34–5
Ford, Henry 2
Formule 1 hotel chain 52–3
fountain pen, lost 8
Four Row Model 25, 65–70, 70–2, 137
Francis, Ric 86
Frankenstein (Shelley) 119
fraud 14–15
Fujitsu 4, 34, 43, 114–15
  alliance with Microsoft 114, 130–3
  Allianz 40–1, 53, 74
  application of templates to services
    85–6, 129–30
  in Australia 37, 135–7
  "la Caixa" 93–4
  electricity monitoring 144
  energy company 77–8
  green data centre 146–7
  Ikeda 122–3, 133–4
  Information@Hand 144
  interactive customer experience
    111–12
  organizational culture 133–5
  Palm Vein Authentication System
    47–8
  Post Office 103
  retail sector 107–8, 125–7
  sustainability 143–4

Reuters 35–6, 56–7, 75–6, 124–5, 146

supply chain 45–6

Toyota 4–5

WH Smith 107–8

Whitbread 60–1, 80–1, 102

Fujitsu University 134

'FUJITSU Way, The' 134, 143

Gaia Symphony 149, 155

Gaia theory 149

General Motors 2

Gladwell, Malcolm 103–4

gas 16

global aggregator of services 75–6, 124–5

Global Supply Chain Management (G-SCM) system 5

globalization 18

Goldman, Lee 103

Gore, Al 149

Goswell, Alan 129–30, 137

government agency 33–5

Gratton, Lynda 121, 125, 129, 130

Great Stink 16–17

Greycoat Placements 141

growing together with the customer 54–6

Hamel, Gary 105

Hamleys 111

heart attacks 102–3

Heathrow Terminal 5 107

help desk 100–1

Hobbs, Rodney 135–7

holistic thinking 138

honour 54

hospitals 88, 103–4, 144–5

hotels 8, 83–4

Conrad Tokyo 141

Formule 1 chain 52–3

Le Saint Géran 79–80

humility 138

igniting purpose 125–7

Ikeda, Toshio 122–3, 133–4

immersion in customer's world 79–81

Inconvenient Truth, An 149

Information@Hand 144

innovation 10, 14, 26, 47, 105–15

co-evolving with partners and suppliers 113–15

continual collaboration with customer 82–3, 106–12

enabling all to contribute to customer's journey 112–13

Four Row Model 25, 65–70, 70–2

sustainability 143, 145

'Innovation hour' 115

interaction 42–3

interactive customer experience 111–12

interconnected whole 145–7

Intergovernmental Panel for Climate Change 149

internet 9, 51–2, 106

invisible excellence 6, 10–12, 16, 26

focus on 59–61

striving to deliver 96–100

Irisys queue management system 108

IT (information technology) 3, 20–1, 141

role in environmental protection 146–7

service wrap 51

Jones, Daniel T. 2, 4

Kamigo engine-machine plant 127–8

Kane, Laura T. 140

Kendall, Peter 45

Kimura, Hiromasa 133

Kim, W. Chan 52–3

Kobayashi, Taiyu 123, 134

Kotler, Philip 52

Kurokawa, Hiroaki 134–5

Le Saint Géran Hotel 79–80

lean production 2–3

lean thinking 2–6
learning, continual 138
Leonard-Barton, Dorothy 148
Levitt, Ted 4, 17–18, 31–2, 135
libraries 140
Lister, David 36, 56, 124
living service 1–27
    adaptation and evolution 14–15, 16,
        26
    balance between people, technology
        and processes 7–10
    and choice 18–20
    elegant simplicity 12–14, 16, 26
    invisible excellence 6, 10–12, 16, 26
    lean thinking 2–6
living service culture see culture
London 16–17
London–Tokyo trip 11–12, 96
long-termism
    service culture 46–8
    sustainability 142, 143–5
Lovelock, James 149

Macroscope 54
Mauborgne, Renée 52–3
Maybach cars 141
meaning, searching for 121
measurement 48
medical representatives (MRs) 58–9
Microsoft 45, 75, 76, 114, 125, 130–3
mind, body and soul 5, 22–5, 30, 64,
    118
mobile phones 1, 81
modularization of products 135–6
music shops 19–20

national culture 135–7
Nippon Roche 58–9
Nokia 45
Nonaka, Ikujiro 57–8

Ohno, Taichi 2
oil 77, 78

Okada, Kanjiro 133
opportunities, turning problems into
    92–4
Oracle 45, 114
organizational culture 133–5
    see also living service culture
organizational silos 120
    breaking 127–35
organizational structure 127–8
ownership vs access 18, 20, 140–1

Palm Vein Authentication System 47–8
partners, co-evolving with 113–15
passbooks 93
Patrick, John 9
people 21–2, 23, 26
    balance between people, technology
        and processes 7–10
    at centre of corporate strategy
        121–2
    ensuring they can realize their own
        and their customers' dreams
        122–7
    as key differentiator 56–7
    putting people at the centre of
        everything 14, 15–16, 39–42
    see also customers; employees
plastics 145
plover 55
portable medical prescription device
    144–5
Post Office 86, 103
Prahalad, C.K. 105
Premier Inns 59, 60
printers, problems with 10, 98–9
Prius car 143
problem-solving 38–9
    Four Row Model 25, 65–70, 70–2
    turning problems into opportunities
        92–4
    see also service development
processes 26
    balance between people, technology
        and processes 7–10